To
Sophie lu[...]
From Den[...]
Jan 23.

Developing the Character of Success

ACHIEVING IN HARD TIMES

Developing the Character of Success
Published by The Conrad Press Limited in the United Kingdom 2021

Tel: +44(0)1227 472 874
www.theconradpress.com
info@theconradpress.com

ISBN 978-1-914913-31-0

Copyright © Esther Mburani, 2021

The moral right of Esther Mburani to be identified as author of this work has been asserted in accordance with the Copyright, Designs and Patents Act 1988.

All rights reserved.

Typesetting and Cover Design by: Charlotte Mouncey, www.bookstyle.co.uk
The Conrad Press logo was designed by Maria Priestley.

Printed and bound in Great Britain by Clays Ltd, Elcograf S.p.A.

Developing the Character of Success

ACHIEVING IN HARD TIMES

Esther Mburani

Acknowledgements

Life is the most valuable asset. I am forever indebted to God for giving me health and wisdom to start and complete this book.

Behind every success, there is a team. My beloved husband, Pastor Harrison Mburani, has been my great support from the start to completing this project. Thank you, Honey, for being part of this project and supporting me in all ways.

I am very grateful to The Conrad Press for publishing this book. I am specifically indebted to Mr James Essinger for overseeing the editing, typesetting, designing and publishing process. Thank you, James, for seeing the value in this book. You are a pleasant person to work with; you make publishing a book an enjoyable adventure. I liked your excellent communication and support at every stage.

I am greatly indebted to Miss Karla Jane Harris for her technical and experienced skills in editing the manuscript. Thank you, Karla, for the invaluable support I received from you and the value you added to this book. It was pleasant to work with you on this project.

When I submitted my manuscript to Bloomsbury Publishing, they could not take it because they already had a closely similar book in progress. However, the feedback I received from Mr Matt James was invaluable. This is part of what he wrote, *'Many thanks for sending over this proposal. From what I've read, it's very interesting and well-written.'* Thank you Matt, for being a person who goes the extra mile to see potential and encourage it to blossom.

I am deeply indebted to my former employer for allowing me the opportunity to lead the programs department and holding the human resources office. Being the head of programs and HR enabled me to observe the relationships between employees' character and their levels of success. This knowledge has been valuable in the process of writing this book.

My appreciation also goes to Mrs Doris Jorgensen, my former boss and mentor. The day I started working with Doris, I learnt that my success or failure depended entirely on me. She exposed me and other staff members to a work environment that made it possible for any one of us to make it to the top. According to Mrs Jorgensen, it was not where you started from that mattered, but where you could reach that was important. Her leadership style gave everyone enough growth room. However, one aspect determined those that grew and those that remained stunted or even withered. One's character determined how far one would succeed. Thank you, Doris; I am ever grateful that I met you.

As you read along, you will see that this book presents a rainbow of experiences. Illustrations are drawn from men and women from all walks of life, from professionals to common men and women you find on the streets, shops, and buses. To all of you whose experiences contributed to the information in this book, I say a big thank you.

Last but not least, thanks to you for purchasing a copy or reading this book. Just one caution, this book does not work like magic. To gain from it, you should consistently practice and implement what it offers.

Esther Mburani   August 2021

To our dear children,
Jabin, Ariella, Netanella and Miracle.
No level of success will be out of reach if you engage the right character and follow the principles in this book.

Contents

Acknowledgements   7

Chapter one
Becoming   15

The four pillars of becoming: Calling, Conviction,
Commitment, and Concentration   21
You must negotiate with life   39
Humility is a critical ally to becoming   41
Shyness, a liability to becoming   44
Shyness as a mild emotional/behavioural disability   45
Overcoming shyness   54

Chapter two
The 'you factor' in thriving beyond hard times   63

Every crisis comes with hidden opportunities   64
You need to discover your position of advantage in a crisis   65
It is not big steps that count, but small ones you
take in the right direction   65
Your background has no power to hold you back   73
No situation is too bad to jump from   75
Hope, the one thing that you should never surrender   76
Be aware of self-pity, the dangerous emotion that works
against you   77
Search for solutions from within you   78
The danger of perceiving other people as a solution
to your problems   79
You have the ability not only to survive but to thrive   80

Take time to build your success	83
Your mind	83
The effect of your mental wellbeing on the capacity to achieve	90
The impact of forgiveness on your success	94
Encourage yourself as often as possible	95
Refuse to carry other people's fears	97
Invest in hope	101
The price of success	102
The currency you use to buy success	103
Know your point of strength	112
Appreciate the chain of success	115
Understanding the value of a zero	121
Even giants need small people around them	133

Chapter three
Pressure, an invaluable ally in achieving success — **142**

The Pressure Pyramid Theory of Success (PPTS)	143
Pressure from your environment	143
Pressure from other people	144
Pressure from self	145
The pressure synergy	147

Chapter four
Determine the person you want to be — **150**

Know your value	150
Self-packaging	151
Be intentional in connecting with God	153
Allow God to take control	156

Chapter five
The personal tree of success model — **159**

The seed and the cracking process	159
The embryo of success	161
Cracking and education processes	162
Cracking and career	168
Cracking in the marriage relationship	170
The usefulness of cracking in parenting	171
Cracking and personal goals	173
Cracking and attaining good health	174
Nurturing your personal tree of success	176
Pillar one: taproot (life)	179
Pillar two: the stem (your brain and the mind)	180
Pillar three: the branches (talent, character, skill)	182
Pillar four: the fruits	183

Chapter six
The power of rejection — **185**

Tapping into the positive power of rejection	185

Chapter seven
The disabling power of trying — **193**

The crippling power of 'trying' on your career	195
Changing you versus changing the job	197
You determine how you live your life	198

Chapter eight
Overcoming crisis — **200**

Preparing for crisis	202
Antidotes to crisis	203

Antidote 1. Develop the faith that defies your crisis	203
Antidote 2: live for a calling that is bigger than the crisis you face.	212
Antidote 3: Make the right decisions at the appropriate time	219
Antidote 4: Accept reality and move forward	226
Antidote 5: Set goals that will keep you focused	227

Chapter nine
The Potter's house experience — **229**

Resilience	229
Shielded by the Potter's hands	231
Endnotes	**234**

Chapter one

Becoming

Success is about becoming and not amassing. The irony about the contemporary way of measuring success is that assessment is based on wealth, achievements, influence, power, status, education, and fame. Although these aspects are essential ingredients of success, they are not adequate to impute success on an individual. Real success goes beyond the tangibles and measurables of life.

Fulfilling and lasting success has more to do with the individual's inner aspect than the external displays. It would be limiting to measure real success by one's bank statement, net worth, investments, or fame. Many excel in these aspects yet live and die as failures.

Success is a product of character. Character is not born, and neither is it inherited; it is made from choice and consistency. Character is like a water tap. Depending on the direction you turn it, it can give you steaming water or ice-cold water. Conditional to the course you turn your character, it can deliver for you success or failure. Therefore, anyone can be successful contingent on the character they assign themselves. Every individual is daily presented with opportunities to make decisions that will culminate either into success or failure. Thus, to succeed is a step by step choice, and likewise, it is to fail.

By developing the right character, people like Harold Hamm, Madam CJ Walker, Oprah Gail Winfrey and Dr Benjamin Solomon Carson Sr, all born on the 'wrong side of life', overcame the numerous hurdles in their way to success.

Harold Hamm was born into poverty. The family needed every hand to help in making ends meet. This meant that young Harold had to participate in family labour. He helped pick cotton barefooted because his family could not afford something as basic as shoes. Though born in abject poverty, he through diligent work curved his way to success and established an oil empire; Continental Resources from nothing but his sweat and labour. The youth whose first job was at a gas station worked his way to becoming a billionaire.

Madam CJ Walker, born to slave parents, fought her way to success. She refused to be content with moderate success. She drove herself into building a successful business that turned her into America's first self-made female millionaire.

Dr Benjamin Carson Sr did not have a promising start in life. In fact, at some point, everything seemed to be going wrong. He was raised in a broken family, had the lowest grades in his class and was on the verge of becoming a knife crime perpetrator. The natural prediction for such a child would have been that he spends his adult life in the ghetto or prison. However, Dr Carson changed his destiny by dropping the loser's habits and adopted the achiever's attitude. With that, he was not only able to overhaul his character but also changed his destiny. He became a world-renowned Neurosurgeon who performed many unprecedented successful Neurosurgeries and developed new ways of treating brain stem tumours. His contribution and inspiration in the medical world remain outstanding. As a result, he received sixty honorary doctorate degrees and was selected by the Library of Congress as one of its living legends. It is unbelievable that a boy who had the lowest grades in class was also housing super brains. It is inconceivable that a boy who was once a member of the gang could achieve that much. Dr Benjamin Carson's life proves that the right character transformed what many would have considered a 'human write-off' into an invaluable asset. His life demonstrates that there is no irredeemable case if the right character is applied as a remedy to attaining success.

Born in poverty and subjected to a hard and abusive childhood did not deter Oprah Winfrey from achieving. Her diligent character has enabled her to move from being an ordinary woman to becoming one of the most famous, wealthy, influential, and successful women of the 21st Century.

None of the above-cited cases had an inheritance or a position of advantage to hinge on their success. They built their success on what was inside them, their character. Success is rooted in the inner values that one lives for and pass on to the next generation.

Supreme success is not the ability to get it right the first time, but the stamina not to give up till you get it right. This is the reason why names like Martin Luther King Jr. continue to echo through generations. It is the inner values that Nelson Mandela stood for that set him apart. His character and the legacy that he left behind made him one of the heroes that history will continue to hold in its pages.

While many people will cite injustice, inequality, lack of resources and opportunities as reasons for their failures, these can be challenged. Available evidence proves that with the right character, no hurdle cannot be surmounted. The biggest obstacle in your path to success is your desire to pursue success on a pre-navigated road. However, at times the road to success will have turns and twists that take you through the jungle of hardships and unfavourable situations. Even then, it is upon you to forge your way out if you do not want to remain stuck in mediocrity.

It is your ability to find the way out of your situation that will make you stand out. Clara B. Williams could not be allowed in the classroom by most of her professors because of her black skin colour. That did not stand in her way to achieving. Instead of quitting, she stood in the hallway and took notes. She eventually graduated and later was awarded an Honorary Doctor of Laws Degree, had a street named after her, and a day issued in her honour and recognition.

While character plays a vital role in determining an individual's success and destiny, many people seem not to realize its importance. However, when you learn that your character brands you, you will start to mind the type of brand you want to become.

The Reader's Digest Oxford Complete Wordfinder defines character as:

'The collective qualities or characteristics, especially mental and moral, that distinguishes a person or a thing.' [1]

Branding creates a distinction and makes something positively stand out from the rest of would-be similar items. The value of the article is often associated with the brand it carries. You do not achieve a higher value than you currently have by changing your wardrobe, car, or job. The collective positive qualities that you adopt into your life will make you complete as an achiever. The acquisition of a few habits that you manipulate to get what you want cannot give you a new identity. Becoming is a process that starts from within. If you desire to change the way you perceive yourself and how others will know you, you need to undertake a character makeover. You need to collectively replace the negative traits with positive qualities. The transformation will occur in the invisible inner space (the mind) and manifest in the visible outer space (the character). When you fill your mind with the right Spirit, people around you will see the transformation in your character. What you are on the inside will influence what you will become on the outside. This will be seen in the character you show as you relate to other people.

'But the fruit of the Spirit is love, joy, peace, longsuffering, kindness, goodness, faithfulness, gentleness, self-control.' [2]

The Spirit that dwells in your mind will dictate the character that you will exhibit. Having the above, as part of the collective values you show to the people you transact with, will accelerate your success. No one is born with such qualities. Anyone can gain them by being intentional.

CASE ILLUSTRATION ONE: THE TILL ATTENDANT

In the year 2019, I went to the store to buy some groceries. After getting what I needed, as any other shopper would usually do, I waited at the till that had a shorter queue. The lady I was following in the queue was probably in her late seventies. From how she was trying to engage the Till Attendant, it was clear that she was the jovial type. The youth, who was probably in his twenties, seemed detached and uninterested in the conversation. He kept his focus on checking out the ladies shopping. While it is common for friendly grandmas to want a chat, this was unique in the way it concluded. As she received her receipt from the youth, she looked him in the face with a radiant smile and said:

'You will do better if you can smile a little bit more.'

I held my breath in fear of how the youth would respond. But, as was the surprise of the granny's loud straightforward advice, so was the impact of the youth's gentle response. Looking in her face, he murmured:

'I will try.'

The lady folded her receipt and, with a smile, wished the youth a nice day.

In June 2020, I went to the same store. As I kept the two-metre distance, my curiosity raised when I saw the same youth at the till. I was pleasantly surprised when he asked in a clear, friendly voice, 'How are you today?' My heart went, wow! Was this the person who just a year ago was so disinterested and detached from his customers? After checking all the items, he bothered to ask if I had a store card, something that he never did the last time he served me—another pleasant surprise. But the best was yet to come; as he handed me the receipt, a gentle smile radiated his face, and he wished me a good day.

That is what becoming is all about. This young man had recognized that his previous character was standing in the way, he was now relating to his customers. Rather than put up a defence, he put on the lady's lenses and re-examined his character. He did not allow false ego to stand in the process of being moulded to perfection. Instead of putting forward excuses, he made an effort to rebrand himself. He was repackaging his character to something that would make his customers want to transact business with him. With such a spirit, this young man may not spend the rest of his working life behind the till. He is on his journey to becoming who he finally wants to be.

Becoming is a process that will allow you to metamorphose from your cocoon, spread your beautiful character and fly to success.

The four pillars of becoming: Calling, Conviction, Commitment, and Concentration

Calling, conviction, commitment, and concentration, make the foundation of your becoming. How satisfied you will be in your engagement will depend on whether you are operating within your calling. The level of your achievement will be determined by the conviction you have in what you do. The output you get will correspond to the degree of your commitment. And your concentration will determine the level of your excellence and perfection. When you order your life around the above four pillars, you operate and achieve at an exceptional level.

When Greta Thunberg realized her calling, she was solid convinced about what she wanted to do, even when she had to start solo. With a homemade poster as her only companion, many would have doubted the sanity of a teenager who sat alone outside the Swedish parliament demanding the impossible. Committed to her calling, she remained resilient during the initial stages of her movement when she had to stand alone as the rest of the world looked on. Soon, her conviction attracted multitudes of students. A cause started by one teenager soon became global and unstoppable. The world could no longer ignore what she was saying.

Greta's commitment, conviction and concentration on her calling has made her one of the most influential persons in the world. At eighteen years, she has power, has influence, has money, and has a cause to live for. Greta Thunberg is not the smartest teen, not the most popular teen, not the wealthiest teen, not the most beautiful teen. What makes her stand out is her solid resolve to fulfil her calling. Because of this, she has been able to achieve at an exceptional level. Before she could even complete high school, she had made herself an indispensable self-appointed advisor to the people who hold power. Her calling has enabled her to carve her space among world leaders. Any world summit on the environment cannot be authentic without her presence. That is the power and influence of a well-articulated calling. Greta has attracted more than six prizes and rejected some which did not resonate with her cause. She has written books, and definitely, she is fixing her footprints on the planet. Her calling has made her a living legend.

Below is a detailed description of how the four pillars of calling, conviction, commitment, and concentration contribute to your becoming.

Calling

Calling and purpose may appear to be the same and have a point of intersection. It is also possible to find the two concepts being used interchangeably. Most people tend to see purpose as the bigger picture of life and say that you can only have one purpose but several callings. However, it is also possible to perceive a calling to be supreme. Under this perception, the calling is regarded as the soul to one's purpose. While the two concepts' ranking may differ, it is crucial to understand that how you perceive them impacts your becoming.

Most scholars, authors, psychologists, sociologists, economists, motivational speakers, and personal coaches emphasize the importance of having a clear purpose as the foundation to success. While that is true, you are likely to achieve more if you know your calling and have a purpose. When you know your calling and have a purpose for your life, you will live your life and perform at an exceptional level.

There can be a mix between calling and purpose. However, you will find it easy to put each of the two drives to beneficial use if you know how they rank, interlink, and influence your life. Calling comes from a higher realm, while purpose can be influenced by the circumstances of life. A calling is internal; it is a drive from within, while purpose can be externally generated. A purpose has more to do with achieving, but the calling is more focused on becoming. Therefore, while the purpose may make you perform, it may lack the power to transform you. Only a calling has the total capacity to move you into becoming and not merely attaining the social, economic, and spiritual ideals you desire.

When you regard your calling as the soul of your purpose, you become meticulously focused on what you want to become. People that run their lives on purpose without a calling may attain possession, power and influence but still feel empty and find no meaning in life. They may have, but not become. However, when you follow your calling and operate with a clear purpose, you position yourself into achieving transforming and satisfying success. Your ability to live the reality of your calling will give value to the wealth, fame, and power you attain.

Your calling is your personal passion that makes you fulfilled and complete. Your calling is what defines you, makes your personal brand and causes you to stand out positively. It makes you feel divinely connected and humanly useful. Acquiring success without a calling to live for can lead to undesirable outcomes. The success that is devoid of calling can destroy you instead of making you. People, celebrities, CEOs, and power giants who run their lives on purpose without a calling are more likely to feel empty and helpless from within.

While purpose can drive you to attain success, it may not equip you to survive what I call *the black hole of success* or the *vacuum point of success*. This is the point where, after achieving it all, you come face to face with the dilemma of, 'what next?' People who get destroyed by their achievements did not have the 'what next' question answered right from the beginning. You can only avoid the black hole of success trap when your life is guided by a calling. When there is no more significant cause to live for than success, attaining success can be the end of a meaningful and exciting life. Success without a calling can lead to a dead end.

When you have achieved it all, it is your calling that will keep life and work exciting. When the excitement of attaining wealth, fame, influence and power has cooled down, your calling will keep you focused, energized, and on course. Even when things temporarily turn in the wrong direction as they will sometimes, it is your calling that will enable you to pull through. A calling will give you something to live for beyond losses, rejections, mistakes, failures, and disappointments bound to come your way in the journey to becoming. In the absence of a calling, success can be a cause of vulnerability. Achieving without a calling can be as damaging and harmful as failure.

Lack of a call-guided life has been part of why people who have acquired wealth, power, pleasure, and fame take their own lives. Once these people attain the tangibles of life, they realize that these do not bring them the happiness they anticipated. When what they have pursued and attained fails to provide meaning for their lives, they do not know how to continue living. They, therefore, decide to bring everything to an end since nothing makes sense to them. They do not see the bigger picture of life and cannot comprehend life's significance beyond pleasing themselves.

On the other hand, having a calling enables you to understand your life as part of the bigger frame. A calling moves you from being self-centred to noticing other people. You get to appreciate that success is not only about what you achieve or lose, but what you become in the process and what you are to others. When you have become, it will not matter how much of the material things that you lose because the real success, which is your character, will remain with you. The character that you develop in the process of becoming is the imperishable asset that you can use to spring back to success at any age, in any place and in any situation. When you have attained the right character, no loss can be significant enough to destroy you because your success is internal.

It is the imperishable asset of character that enabled Joe Biden to become president of United States of America after trying for thirty-two years and losing twice. While many at his age would have given up the dream and settled into retirement, Joe Biden took his presidential oath at the age of seventy-eight years. Thus, becoming the oldest person ever elected the president of the United States of America.

While purpose may expire, a calling lives on. It is through your calling that you can irreversibly write your life on earth's pages.

'Then I heard a voice from heaven say, write this: 'Blessed are the dead who die in the Lord from now on'. 'Yes', says the Spirit, 'they rest from their labor, for their deeds will follow them.' [3]

When you live for a calling, you do not only attain success, but your legacy lives on. This is why names like Nelson Mandela, Martin Luther King, Martin Luther the Reformer, Ellen G. White, Charles Wesley, Florence Nightingale and Mother Teresa are still given a relevant place in our times. The good works that these people achieved by pursuing their calling remains an inspiration to many, although the individuals are no more. When you live for a calling, it becomes impossible to feel empty because the more you do, the more you become. The more you give to humanity, the more you feel complete.

What makes a calling to be of more worth than a stand-alone purpose is the feeling of completeness that it brings to your inner being. There tend to be two aspects of you: the external you and the internal you. A purpose can appease the exterior you, but only a call will have the power to satisfy the inner you. It is the inner you that gives meaning to your life. It does not matter how much you have on the external display; happiness will remain an illusion if the inner you feels empty.

If I use the analogy of a compass and a map, your calling would be your compass, and your purpose would be the map. You need to follow the compass to make meaningful use of the map and benefit from it. In other words, your calling is the one that gives direction to your purpose. You are, therefore, able to excel holistically when you are operating within your calling and with a clear purpose. It should be encouraging to know that everyone has a calling. A person that bothers to find his calling and aligns it with purpose opens his door to excellence.

Finding your calling

Although people tend to limit a calling to direct divine engagements, a calling can be in any engagement of your passion that brings honour to God and benefits mankind. A calling cannot be limited to clergy or services that are directly linked to the church. It is much broader than that. God gives different people differing abilities to do various things for His glory and the benefit of mankind. The human needs require more than what can be provided by those that are in direct church service. Therefore, God being the provider and sustainer of mankind, needs and uses people in various capacities to cause happiness, harmony and sustain His creation. This is why He calls some to be farmers, others to be politicians and some to the medical field, while others He places them in business and so on.

'There are different kinds of gifts, but the same Spirit. There are different kinds of service, but the same Lord. There are different kinds of working, but the same God works all of them in men. Now to each one, the manifestation of the Spirit is given for the common good.' [4]

The point is, a calling can be in any discipline or field. Therefore, living a call-focused life does not limit your areas of engagement. Anything that you are passionate about, glorifies God and makes humanity better can be your calling. Your calling can be in politics, medicine, business, teaching, social work, farming, or anything else that passionately drives you. The litmus test is that what you do makes you feel at your best, does not conflict with divine principles and benefits mankind. Anything that does not violate God's immutable law, attracts higher meaning to your existence and makes mankind better, qualifies as a calling.

Your calling remains the same in life; only your means of responding to it will change. For instance, it is possible to respond to the calling of alleviating human suffering by first being a businessman and then being a philanthropist. You can also do both concurrently.

When you find your calling, your worldview and perception of work and success get transformed. When the two are considered drivers of success, purpose tends to be inadequate when it operates on the ideology of 'the end, justifying the means.' Many people that use purpose as the only driver to achieve success tend to run on a narrow spectrum. The focus seems to be on what is to be achieved, and anything else may not count much. The rightness of the means used, the path taken, and what is done may not morally bother the individual pursuing success using purpose as his only drive. Ethics and morality are at high risk of being pushed aside or ignored when purpose alone takes the lead. Values may be situationally applied by the person who has his eyes fixed on purpose alone. For instance, an employer whose purpose is to earn a million pounds in twelve months may find no problem overworking and underpaying his employees. In fact, he is likely to perceive it as good business acumen when he can spend less and earn more. Such success that is achieved on a narrow spectrum may remain superficial and powerless to cause character transformation.

It is, however, different when you pursue success by following a calling. A calling informs and shapes your core values. You perceive what you become to be of more significance than what you accumulate. Your engagements cease to be a means of only achieving some ends. You seek to become a better person. You are intentional about how each engagement will shape and strengthen your character. You get to look beyond the paycheques, the profits, the shares in the stock market and the investments. Your spectrum of seeing things gets broader; in everything you do and achieve, you see people, family, humanity, and God.

When you perceive what you do as a calling, and not only a means to an end, your goals and expectations get redefined. The new perception changes your values, and your accountability bar gets raised. You see other obligations beyond yourself and your family. You feel duty-bound beyond paying your bills, paying your employees, and paying the taxman. You see yourself through the eyes of humanity, and it becomes your self-imposed obligation to make the world a better place. Because of this, people like Mark Zuckerberg and his wife, Priscilla Chan, can share ninety-nine percent of their wealth with humanity. Calling drives Bill and Melinda Gates to be at the forefront of causes that affect humanity. The sense of calling gives self-made millionaires like Oprah Winfrey a huge heart to share what they have earned with their own sweat with the rest of the world.

A calling is not synonymous with suffering. Living your call does not mean that you have to be miserable and in want, as some tend to suggest. Following your call can lead to gaining wealth, power, influence and even fame. However, when you are guided by calling, you use what you gain to propagate a more significant good. You use your power to protect and not cause harm or suffering, and you use your influence to generate good.

Nelson Mandela provides an excellent example of a life lived according to one's calling. While it took him twenty-seven years of harsh imprisonment to liberate South Africa, he used his power, influence and fame for the good of humanity. He was satisfied with one term in the president's office and refrained from using his power to cause revenge. He used his fame and influence to heal a country that was wounded and divided by apartheid. Mandela's pursuance of justice and equality was a calling that he was ready to live for at all costs.

Following and realizing a call does not come easy. There must be opportunity cost, something you are willing to give away to attain what you desire. Other than that, dependent on your personal convictions, your calling can be a means that leads you to higher material, social, economic, and spiritual attainments. For example, Abraham, also known as the father of the faithful, was well endowed in wealth, power, and influence even as he followed his divine calling. Therefore, you can attain more tremendous success by pursuing and living your calling.

Some people easily find their calling. It comes almost like an intuition; they know what they are called to be in life without any struggle. If you are such an individual, you right from the beginning knew where you were heading. People who easily find their calling do not require a career master, a mentor, or even a coach to help them identify what they want to become in life. Such people are hard, or even impossible, to confuse. They do not get mixed up regarding who they are and why they are here. These individuals clearly know where they stand and where they want to reach. While the world around them may offer various enticing options and attractive alternatives, they do not waver from their calling. They faithfully pursue what they desire without looking to the left or the right. For example, an individual who has a calling in helping suffering humanity may respond by taking a career in medicine. However, because of his passion for the suffering, he may decline a job offer from Johns Hopkins Hospital and prefer to work with Médecins Sans Frontières - Doctors Without Borders. In such an example, it is the calling to help those in need that influences the individual's service of compassion.

When you act within your calling, success begins to flow your way. When your career is within your calling, your outlook on success gets transformed. You turn tasks into a passion. Whether you are the CEO of your own company or are volunteering, passion becomes the hallmark of what you do. The power flowing from your passion attracts people to transact business, partner, or relate with you. Positive passion attracts good relationships, and your success largely depends on your excellent connections with people. I will give a brief example.

Recently, I went to post mail from a newly opened post office shop. My business in the shop was to have the letter posted and leave. However, I was amazed when the gentleman behind the counter asked me if my daughter liked the balloons I bought from his shop two weeks ago. That was a surprise; how many shopkeepers randomly ask a customer about their satisfaction with a minor item bought half a month ago? By asking that question, the shopkeeper communicated several things that any customer would appreciate. All the following were embedded in his simple question. First, 'I remember you.' Second, 'You are essential to my business.' Third, 'I am not only interested in your money, but I also care about your satisfaction.' Fourth, 'I can see beyond the transaction to the recipient, who is your child.' And last, 'I am willing to take suggestions to provide a better service.' This shopkeeper was connecting with me, his client because he perceived his business as a calling. He was doing more than running a profitable business. He was, through his trade, responding to the call to meet the needs of others. That is what gave him the passion for what he was doing.

While there is a category that will quickly know their calling, not all people will easily identify what they are called to become in life. If you are one of such people, there is no need to worry. Though it may take you a journey, you will eventually know your calling if you bother to find it. It is at the point that you discover your calling that you start to become. Your willingness to become the person you have the potential to be will determine your success level.

It is possible and okay to try a couple of things in the process of finding your calling. However, the key indicator that will let you know that you have not yet identified your calling will be the lack of inner satisfaction. Even though you may have a purpose, you will experience gaps in your life if you are operating outside your calling. People who fail to become what they have the potential to be will feel the void but suppress it. At times, such people may start the search but stop before finding what they are looking for. These fellows are fond of 'I can't be bothered' attitude. People under this category will feel their calling but decide to abandon it because it demands more than they are willing to invest.

On the other hand, the people that become what they have the potential to be never stop the search until they are where they want to be. These perceive their journey to becoming as an investment. They become aware of the fact that aligning their calling with their purpose increases their motivation and satisfaction. Living within your calling goes beyond having money, power, and influence. These aspects that many people consider to be icons of success do not necessarily satisfy the inner desire to become. Only responding to one's actual calling does that.

Another mark of a calling is that it brings a connection between you and the higher realm. When you are operating within a calling, you feel that you are meeting more than your own needs. You feel a kind of connection between what you do and serving humanity. It is the element of being relevant to other people that brings you inner satisfaction. When you respond to your calling, you will feel at peace with your maker.

'Whatever you do, work at it with all your heart, as working for the Lord, not for human masters.' [5]

The importance of operating within your calling is that the motivation to do what you do gets influenced by higher values. The values you hold will enable you to develop a mindset that cannot be discouraged. Operating within a calling gives you the resistance not to succumb to discouragements. It is that resistance that will make you an achiever in situations where others are failing and quitting. When you operate within your calling, you move from being an average performer to becoming a star.

Your calling will become your lifestyle, and your goals will be the means to achieve it. This means that your calling is bigger than your career or your job. While a career can be stand-alone, a calling is life-encompassing. For instance, if my calling is to positively touch people's lives through writing, this will influence how I live. It will inform how I think, my plans, where I live, what I read, how I work, how I use my resources, how I socialize and relate, how I eat and even how I sleep.

Choosing your calling gives you a natural niche over others. When you gravitate towards what you are passionate about, work ceases being an obligation and transforms into a delight. Instead of work draining your strength, it energises you. You look forward to doing things instead of dreading them. Each morning and each day is filled with anticipation about what you want to accomplish. In short, operating within your calling enables you to develop a winning attitude in what you engage in. Besides that, your joy and enthusiasm to work become contagious to all who interact with you. People will enjoy your services because you are not merely doing a job, but you share a part of who you are with the rest of the world.

Finding your calling is a vital aspect of your process of becoming. It does not matter how long it takes, and the age at which you find it is immaterial. Never settle into doing something that leaves you feeling a void, feeling unfulfilled or dissatisfied. When you settle into doing something that is not within your calling, you deny yourself the opportunity to grow in your success. However, when you operate within your calling, it may be challenging in the beginning, but you will eventually make huge leaps.

Conviction

The Collins English dictionary defines conviction as *'a firmly held belief or opinion.'* Knowing your calling will not do much to make you the person you want to become if you do not firmly believe in it. When you have a calling, you need to develop absolute faith in it. When you are not convinced about what you want to become, you make yourself available for sabotage by people, situations and even yourself.

In the absence of conviction, following your calling can be a challenge or even an impossibility. You probably have heard people who say that 'I wanted to become this or that, but...' the 'but' comes because the person lacked absolute faith in what he wanted. When there is no faith in an engagement, there cannot be results. Each time you seek something new or something unusual, you have to face and deal with the numerous 'what ifs'. You cannot respond to your calling and remain faithful to it unless you learn to keep the 'what if' button in your mind muted. This does not mean that you take irrational decisions. It means that after adequately thinking through what you believe is your calling, you need to shut out the afterthoughts. This is because, most of the time, afterthoughts come as a result of fear. When you respond to your calling, you may experience fear because of the uncertainties involved, the challenges anticipated, and even the price or cost you have to pay. This fear causes many people who know what they want to remain stuck in doing the things they are not satisfied with. The fear of taking on the calling makes many people that would be successful to never become. The challenge faced by many in their journey to becoming is not the lack of knowledge on what they should do, but rather the absence of conviction to follow through with what they know.

When you have conviction, it will not matter how far you have gone in the wrong direction; you will have the courage to stop and start walking in the right direction. You will not be threatened by the challenges ahead, and neither will what you have prevent you from attaining what you can be. The presence of conviction will enable you to turn your eyes from what you are and focus on what you have the potential to become. The point is, it is impossible to respond and remain faithful to a calling unless you have total conviction in it. The absence of conviction will provide room for doubt. When you allow doubt to reign in your mind, you block your own path to success. You need to realize success in your mind before you can live it. This makes conviction a significant pillar in your journey to becoming.

Commitment

The Collins English dictionary defines commitment as *'dedication to a cause of principle.'* You do not excel by engaging in everything that shows potential. When you look at animals, some are opportunistic feeders. Animals that fall under this category are generalist when it comes to what they eat. Because these animals know that they can feed on many things, they never focus. Some may keep hopping or moving from place to place. As a result, they spend more time running than eating. A rabbit provides an excellent example of an opportunistic feeder in the animal world. When you find a rabbit in its natural environment, you will see it nibble on one thing, hop to another, and jump to the next. By the nature of its feeding, a rabbit does not leave any mark where it has been feeding. This is because it never focuses long enough to make an impact.

In the rabbit's mind, the next bush provides the best feed. Possessing the rabbit's mindset in terms of not being focused, will stand in your way to becoming because you will always be on the lookout for what you can try next. You will spend most of your time trying one thing after another. You will change from one job to another and take various courses that you do not put to good use. A hopping mindset will cause you to miss your calling because you will be chasing after everything that comes to your sight and other people's dreams.

If you desire to become what you have the potential to be, you must be willing to commit to what you believe to be your calling. Using the animal example again, animals that specialise in what they eat have an advantage over the rest because they get less competition. That is the same thing with you. Life offers numerous routes to success. It is impossible to succeed if you want to take all of them. You must commit to the route that will best lead you to where you want to reach. Changing from one course to another has various disadvantages. First, it will cost you more time to get where you want to be. Secondly, it will be more exhausting. Third, you are more likely to feel frustrated if you keep changing, and the possibilities of burn-out become higher. And lastly, you may never reach because on the journey to becoming, not all routes lead to the same destination. While many people know what they deeply desire, it is the ability to be committed that draws the line between those that succeed and those that do not.

It is a common saying that 'there is no straight path to success'. This means that you cannot attain success without meeting challenges. However, what marks the difference between the people who succeed and those who do not is commitment. People who fail to realize their potential back off when the mountains get too steep to climb. However, those that succeed remain committed and climb their mountains one step at a time. People without commitment turn back when they cannot see beyond the wall that stands between them and success. Those that are committed remind themselves that tunnels can be dug through walls. People that are not committed will find more than enough reasons why things cannot work out. Those who are committed will see no reasons strong enough to stop them from pursuing what they desire.

Being committed puts you in charge of your own life and destiny because you do not allow any force to derail you. Conversely, the absence of commitment provides others with a license to manipulate you into doing things to their advantage and to your detriment. When you are not committed, people can sway you in any direction that benefits them. They find you to be an accessible tool they can use as a ladder to climb to their success. Being committed means that you devote your attention, thoughts, time, and resources to what you want to become. It means that you avoid doing things because someone else is doing them, and they look promising. It means that you remain focused on pulling out your own success and do it in your own way.

Concentration

You will always stand out when you specialise. Concentration has been defined as *'to focus all one's attention, thoughts, or efforts.'* However, it is impossible to specialise unless you learn to focus your mind. This is a principle that cuts across all disciplines in life. Concentration is key in attaining and achieving above average. In addition, the ability to narrow your scope to what you want will give you the benefit of devoting your time and resources to the most rewarding cause.

While the world will offer unlimited options, you must choose to concentrate on enhancing what you want to become. You will never find it richly rewarding if you scatter your attention. Knowing a bit of everything does not make you useful in a specific or significant manner. If you notice, the world is not in lack of people who know a bit of everything. The global shortage is on deep specialisation in specifics. The deeper you go, the more universally relevant you will become.

Concentration can be looked at in the way of being able to give undivided and prolonged attention. However, it can also mean the ability to align your purpose, goals, plans and thoughts in your call's direction and the person you want to be.

You must negotiate with life

You do not have to take what life offers you. There is so much in life than what you currently have. You can get a better deal when you intentionally and purposefully negotiate on what you desire and deserve. Life will place you in an initial position, but that does not have to be your station in life. The journey to becoming involves active negotiation at every stage until you are satisfied that you have reached the point where you feel complete.

To negotiate your way to becoming, you must understand the variables and immutables of life. Examples of variables are character, income levels, environment, skills, and education. Examples of life's immutables are race, death, parents, siblings, family, seasons, and weather. Variables in life are things that you have the power to influence, determine or change. If you want to be effective, you must focus your negotiations on the variable domain. For instance, being born poor is a variable because you can change that. You do not have to remain poor for the rest of your life. A good percentage of wealthy people were once poor, and a reasonable number of billionaires come from poor backgrounds.

On the other hand, immutables of life are things that you do not have control over. You cannot change those things from being what they are. A good negotiator will not spend time trying to negotiate with the immutables of life. Instead, he accepts them and uses them as stepping stones or takes them in a stride as he strives to grasp what he has control over.

For instance, it is futile to try and change your race or deny who your family is. Instead, you achieve better when you find ways in which your race can work for you. Many people have cited race as a significant hindrance to their becoming. Smart negotiators understand race's immutability and take it in a stride or use it as a stepping stone to becoming who they want to be. Key among these is Mr Barack Obama, who never tried to defend who he was. Throughout his two terms in the office, he was content to belong to a black race. While many people allege that they cannot get a job promotion because of their race, Mr Obama convinced the world's superpower to choose him as president twice. The difference between Mr Obama and others who do not become what they want to be is the side on which they focus their negotiations. Those that fail in life spend time focusing on changing the unchangeables while ignoring to change the changeables.

While your character is the most critical asset you need to

succeed, it is also the most mouldable variable in your life. You have complete control and power over the character that you want to have. It is possible to replace aspects of your character that stand in your way with character traits that will propel you to become the person you desire to be. A school of thought asserts that you cannot change your temperament based on the reasoning that temperament is a part of your biology. While that is a defendable position, becoming an active negotiator involves mastering the art of manoeuvring around what stands in your way. That includes your temperament. For instance, while you may not change from being a sanguine, you can keep under control aspects of your sanguine personality that hold you back from achieving. For example, being disorganized and bad listening are part of sanguine's negative traits, which can undermine your efforts to become. However, when you are an active negotiator, you will not be comfortable with what your temperament offers you. You will push yourself into becoming better organized and a good listener. You will realize that becoming successful involves having good relationships with other people. Good listening is a critical skill in achieving that.

In short, if you want to become, you do not use nature's unchangeables to excuse or defend your situation. Instead, you use your negotiating power to replace changeable primary conditions with ideal circumstances that support and enhance your progress to become.

Humility is a critical ally to becoming

Humility teamed with wisdom begets greatness. To become a great person, you need to be a humble individual. Success is a journey that involves knocking on closed and, at times, locked doors. While you will have the ability to personally open some of the doors that lie in your path, you will need the cooperation of the persons that are keeping the keys to unlock the locked doors in your way. Humility is soft power. It makes the people you interact with support and respect you while they feel valued. When correctly applied, humility appeals to other people to offer you the collaboration and partnership you need on your way to becoming. It also enables you to benefit from people's critiques and make situations work for you. You are likely to have people support you to get what you want and reach where you want to be when humility is part of your character.

Humility is not synonymous with weakness. While humility opens doors for you, weakness slams them in your face. Humility is not the same as allowing others to take advantage of you. Neither is it putting up a show to manipulate others to get what you want. It is all about respecting yourself and treating others with respect. When appropriately engaged, humility can permeate obstacles in your way and create a smooth path for you where the arrogant are hitting the walls. It is an excellent tool in defusing opposition, conflict and turning sabotage into cooperation. I will give a short illustration to explain.

It was one of those typical hot days in August, and my friend was on a bus coming from a hospital appointment. There were no more free seats on the bus, so she stood in the space for buggies. Suddenly, her peace was interrupted when an elderly lady seated next to where she was standing shouted:

'Do you mind opening that window?'

Irrespective of the commanding and arrogant tone, my friend responded.

'No problem,' as she reached out for the window. After trying, she could not figure out how to open the bus window. She turned to the old lady who was visibly observing her and said to her,

'Sorry, I can't figure out how to open this window.'

The lady responded with disdain:

'You have never opened a window in your entire life, have you? Okay, here, I will tell you how to open it.'

While my friend felt the need to tell the lady how her character was obnoxious, she changed her mind. She decided to respond in a manner that maintained her dignity and show the lady her folly in a respectful manner. This was what she did; she carefully followed the lady's commanding instructions and opened the window. By this time, all passengers had their attention drawn to what was happening between the two ladies (my friend is black, and the old lady was white). My friend could see that the racial aspect made both white and black passengers keenly interested. She looked at the lady with a genuine smile and, in a calm and friendly voice, said;

'Ma'am, I have opened several windows in my life. But this was the first time to open a bus window. I rarely travel on a bus.'

When she turned, she could see that her smile had become contagious; all the passengers smiled at her in a manner that seemed to say, 'well done'. The old lady took the lesson with grace. When the passenger seated next to her alighted, she invited my friend to take the seat. Her attitude changed, and she did her best to start and maintain a conversation. That was one encounter between arrogance and humility, and no doubt the latter prevailed.

Shyness, a liability to becoming

I have on several occasions heard people associate themselves with shyness as if it was a positive trait. Probably, you too have heard or maybe even uttered statements such as: 'I am a very shy person and don't like the limelight'. Unfortunately, while some people will say such a statement thinking that it is a strength and a sign of humility, the opposite is true. The truth and sad reality is that shyness is a huge liability. Admitting that you are a shy person has the same damaging effect on your personality as confessing that you are a timid person. The dictionary defines the word '*shy*' as:

'Not at ease in the company of others, easily frightened, timid, to draw back from doing something through lack of confidence.' [6]

While it is possible to misname shyness for humility, the two traits are fundamentally different in how they impact your progress to success. While shyness will continuously draw you back and curtail your advancement, humility will enable you to advance. As you may have already realized or will come to realize, there are numerous hurdles you will have to deal with on your way to success. While humility is a crucial trait that will surround you with the support you need to overcome hurdles and advance in achieving your goals, shyness will achieve the opposite for you. Shyness will disable you from seizing numerous opportunities for you to grow, shine and excel. It will rob you of self-confidence, one of the crucial character traits you need to push forward and achieve.

Shyness as a mild emotional/behavioural disability

Valid, under the health and legal definitions, shyness will not pass as a disability. However, when you consider its capacity to disable the individual's ability to fully function at optimum potential, shyness does qualify as a hidden form of disability. The Wikipedia Free Encyclopaedia defines disability to be:

'Any condition that makes it more difficult to do certain activities or interact with the world around them. These conditions or impairment may be cognitive, developmental, intellectual, mental, physical, sensory or a combination of multiple factors.' [7]

From the above definition, shyness qualifies as a form of disability because it makes it more difficult for the person experiencing it to interact. Disability is any condition that puts you out of control of what you would like to do, feel, or be, limits your abilities in terms of what you can achieve. Most of the time, shy people do not like the character they display when experiencing shy episodes. In fact, they feel helpless inside and even suffer mental torment because of how they behaved. They feel embarrassed for doing the opposite of what they would have desired to do. It is common for shy sufferers to regret their disliked behaviour which they seem to be helpless about. Any situation that limits you from acting the way you would have desired puts you out of control.

The World Health Organisation recognizes disability as:

'any condition of the body or the mind that makes it more difficult for the person with the condition to do certain activities (activity limitation) and interact with the world around them (participation restriction).' [8]

It is unrefutable knowledge that shyness limits an individual's participation. Many people did not take part in what would have been life-changing opportunities because shyness stood in their way. Thousands missed turning points to become successful just because they felt too shy to step forward, too shy to make a move, too shy to speak, too shy to act or too shy to participate. The fact that shy people do not like what they do and yet feel powerless to change makes them experience inner vulnerability. Extreme shyness can make one portray awkward behaviour that injures the person's self-esteem.

Shyness will not make you a better person because it inhibits you from stepping forward and opening the doors of success that stand before you. For example, it is possible to miss a better job opportunity because you are too shy to ask the manager for a promotion. You may have missed the secret love of your life because while shyness held you back from approaching her, another man proposed. You may have missed that business deal because you were shy to step forward and push for it. Someone else may have taken advantage of your ideas because you were shy to implement them. Someone may have offered the same suggestion that you knew but could not share because of shyness, and they got a better job. In short, shyness is detrimental because it will cause you to run away from new opportunities instead of reaching out and grasping them.

While it is natural to feel the need to hold back and be more comfortable keeping in familiar waters. You cannot attain success unless you are willing to step into places that make you feel odd and uncomfortable. It is impossible to attain substantial achievement if you are not ready to leave your cosy corner and step into what will cause you to feel awkward. While success is a comfortable place, the road leading there can be very uncomfortable and bumpy. One of the things that successful people had to overcome was the drawback force of shyness. They had to develop the stamina and courage of replacing shyness with confidence. While some successful people may carry the shy character trait, they do not allow it to hinder their success. They know how to keep this negative trait under control. They do not give it the liberty to stand between them and the success that they desire to achieve. They may never entirely detach from shyness, but they eliminate its adverse effects by practicing what I will call *'selective shyness.'* You may not find this term in any other book because I am using it functionally.

This means that while the individual is still carrying the shy character trait, he can overrule it in situations that matter. Therefore, selective shyness is controlled shyness. Great people like Rosa Parks or even President Abraham Lincoln are said to have carried the shy character trait. However, they kept this trait under check and never allowed it to reign where matters were at stake. They were masters in replacing shyness with confidence whenever stakes were high. They did not find problems to convert their soft nature into the solidness of rock and stand unmoved when situations warranted it.

Several successful people have learned the art of taming shyness. You may have come across successful people who appear shy in places that do not matter. Such people may prefer to take the back seat at the function that does not impact their success. These people will sit amidst a bubbly group of colleagues, and apart from a shy, gentle smile on their face, no one will hear their word unless they are prompted to speak. They may want to go unnoticed, and they dread pompous introductions by other people because such makes them feel uncomfortable.

However, when you find the same person in a situation that matters to his success, he will portray a totally different personality. For instance, at a business meeting, he will take a conspicuous seat. He will be proactive in introducing himself to other business executives. He will passionately share what his company does and look for new business partnerships without allowing his character weakness to hold him back. When in meetings, he will talk, and others will listen because he speaks wisdom. However, when you meet the same man in the corridor on his way home, he may not say much apart from offering you a shy smile as he passes by you on his way to the car parking lot. Such a man may be undeniably shy but will not allow shyness to restrict his potential. When it is time to act and achieve, he will summon all the confidence it takes to fully participate and influence the outcome that he desires to see. People who practice selective shyness will not go around drumming the fact that they are shy. This is because they are aware of the fact that shyness is a liability to their success and never will it at any time convert into an asset.

Shyness has a great capacity to neutralize potential. Millions of people with excellent prospects, presented with ample opportunities, end up mediocre or even failures because they allow shyness to hold them back. One simple but very crucial truth that you can take from this part of the book is that there is no point in life when shyness will work for you. It will always be against you. Therefore, every time you want to advance and feel shyness tightening its strings around you, you must sever the cord.

Unless you press the resolve button and push forward into the freedom of confidence, the next feeling that you will have to deal with is regret. A moment of shyness can be the space that determines the celebration of your success or regretting your failure. For example, in an interview, the shy mannerisms communicate to the panel that you are unsure of yourself and, therefore, unfit for the job. I have been on several interviewing panels. It was always sad to see people who had the knowledge, miss the job because they allowed shyness to stand in their way to convince the panel that they had what it takes to deliver. This was mainly with the jobs that required someone to be upfront in networking with other partners and securing business partnerships. However, it was surprising to see candidates who did not have as much knowledge get the job because of their ability to demonstrate that they can deliver.

While according to its capacity to inhibit participation and engagement, shyness can be perceived as a form of disability. It is a temporary form. The positive side is that you do not have to remain shy for the rest of your life. You can overcome that negative character trait or learn how to keep it under control so that it does not stand in your way to achieving success.

While there may be different views among scholars on whether shyness is genetic or is learned, the fact is that no baby drops from its mother's womb when it is shy. Professor Bernardo J. Carducci, the director of *Shyness Research Institute at Indiana University*, also shared this view. The belief that shyness is not genetic is premised on the fact that shyness comes with self-awareness. Several studies have proved that babies are not self-aware until after a few months of their birth. This makes shyness to be a character trait that is learned and acquired as one goes through life. Therefore, as the saying goes, 'what is learned can be unlearned'. If you learned to become shy, you can unlearn to be shy. A baby learns to be shy the same way he would have learned to be confident.

While shyness is influenced by parenting, environment, culture, exposure, and general prevailing situations, it can also be self-imposed. For instance, without thinking about the long-term damaging impact of shyness, one can claim to be shy as a means of escaping unwanted responsibilities. For example, a child who does not want to take a leading role in the school concert will use shyness as an escape route. An employee who does not want to do extra work will claim to be shy to avoid getting involved in preparing the presentation for the board. However, if you are in the game of using shyness as a shield, you need to remember that the mind will always believe what you tell it. In fact, your mind can convert your false claims into reality. If you are fond of using shyness as an excuse, you risk having this negative trait take root in your life.

Shyness is a first cousin of fear in the sense that they both have a significant capacity to stand in your way to act at your full potential. In fact, uncontrolled or untamed shyness can beget fear to perform, fear to act, fear to relate, fear to confront situations that stand in your way and fear to excel. Therefore, the way fear is detrimental to your achievement is the same way shyness can hinder you from attaining success.

Shyness can also come as a result of other people mislabelling you. For example, parents and teachers are prone to misunderstand a child's quietness for shyness. Your friends are likely to mistake your silence for shyness. Such mislabelling can cause you to adapt shyness as your character even when you were initially not a shy person. For purposes of clarity, being quiet, calm, and reserved does not necessarily mean that you are shy, as some people tend to think. When you are an introvert, it should not mean that you are automatically shy. Such personality blanket cataloguing can cause people to misunderstand you or mislead you. Therefore, do not hesitate to correct people who want to hang around your neck the *'shy'* disabling character tag.

Shyness and humbleness are not the same. They are fundamentally different. A shy person is not necessarily a humble person. In fact, a shy person can be arrogant, rebellious, and evil in attitude and actions. Therefore, shyness should not be mistaken for purity, sincerity, or goodness. In the Bible, King Saul's story presents an example of a shy king who turned out to have an evil personality.

'But when they sought him, he could not be found. Therefore, they inquired of the LORD further, 'Has the man come here yet?' And the LORD answered, 'There he is, hidden among the equipment. So they ran and brought him from there.' [9]

While King Saul was too shy to the extent that he tried to avoid his own coronation ceremony, he later in his reign stood tall in doing evil. He became arrogant, disobeyed God's instruction, murdered innocent people, tried to kill his own son, and hunted David as if he was a beast.

If you find it confusing to draw a line between shyness and humility, here are the significant differences.

Key differences between shyness and humility

Shyness is a personality weakness that is associated with

self-doubt. When people realize that you are shy, they may not want to invest their confidence in you. This was the case with Saul. After being brought from his hiding place and pronounced king over Israel, some of the people who witnessed his behaviour refused to accept him as king.

'They did not give Saul the customary gifts people give to a new king. They said, 'He was hiding in the supplies. How is he going to lead us?' [10]

Shyness will cause others to question your suitability, credibility, and authority. Therefore, if you want to win people's trust, you need to replace shyness with confidence. While shyness will cause you to feel helpless, humility is soft power comparable to the power of a chain. Unlike other pieces of metal, the chain presents the highest level of flexibility. What makes the chain unique from other works of metal is its flexibility without breaking. You can turn the chain in several directions and adjust it to fit particular functions without altering its shape. Now, the flexibility of the chain does not reduce its power, effectiveness, or functioning. The chain can bend and form into any shape, yet it is the most challenging piece of metal to break. The simple secret of the power of the chain lies in its numerous flexible joints. The weak joints enable the chain to adapt to various functions without being broken, adjusted or reshaped. While the chain may present a weak form, it is this same form that makes it have comparably superior strength over other forms and shapes. This is why a chain that weighs less can handle a load much more than its weight. So is humility. It gives you the ability to survive in conditions that would have otherwise been overwhelming for you. Humility gives you the advantage to succeed in situations where others are failing.

While shyness may hinder people from partnering with you in business, most people will feel drawn to work with a person who displays confidence with humility. The opposite of humility is pride; nobody wants a business partner who is proud or arrogant. Therefore, while humility will draw people to work with you, shyness will make people distance themselves from you. This is because nobody wants a business partner who displays a timid personality or presents a persona that communicates a lack of confidence. Shyness and humility are also different in the sense that while shyness makes people treat you with disdain, humility attracts respect. I will use the life of Moses to illustrate this principle.

While Moses is recorded as the humblest person on earth at his time of living, he was also unmatched in leadership abilities.
'Now, the man Moses was very humble, more than all men who were on the face of the earth.' [11]

Moses' humility presents a character trait contrary to what many people expect to be a leader's core strength. The Pharaohs are historically known to have been among the most powerful rulers of the time. Yet, despite being humble, armed with humility, persistence and dependency on God, Moses championed the Israelites' freedom and prevailed against the Pharaoh.

Another marked difference between shyness and humility is that while shyness will encourage people to take advantage of you, humility will command respect. People tend to love humble leaders and follow them out of respect. However, when you are a shy person, you may find it hard to attract followers, and even when you do, there is a higher chance of losing them to someone confident.

Overcoming shyness

Various studies indicate that character is shaped by both nature and nurture. Like many other aspects of your life, character can be trained, manipulated, and influenced by applying deliberate actions. Success can be achieved when you eliminate negative character traits that stand in your way and replace them with positive character traits. Shyness is one of those character traits that are a liability and are likely to stand in your way to success.

Below are practical suggestions that can help to stop shyness from standing in your way to becoming.

1. Keep a positive mind: Shyness starts in your mind. Your external world is shaped by your inner world- the world in your mind. You become shy because of what you perceive in your inner world. What you envision in your mind become your reality when you interact with people. Shyness is a premeditated emotion. You do not feel shy when you face a situation or when you meet a person. The shyness emotion is created in your mind before the encounter. When you meet the person, you just implement what is already existing in your mind. For example, if you feel shy about meeting your boss for the first time, you will act shy when you finally meet him. However, when you encourage your mind to feel excited about meeting your boss, you will feel confident when you hold your hand out to greet him.

When you are insecure in the inner world (your mind), you emerge in the external world (reality) as a timid person.

Conversely, being secure in the inner world will empower you to relate to the external world with confidence.

2. Think positively about who you are: Shyness starts with the negative thoughts that you allow in your mind. Negative thoughts about yourself, other people, and situations are likely to make you face life in a shy mode. It is, therefore, crucial that you cultivate positive thinking. For instance, many people tend to think negatively about some aspects of their lives. You need to stop being bothered by your skin colour or body shape. Instead, take whatever you have as a positive and celebrate it. If you are packaged in black skin, love yourself. If you are wrapped in red skin colour, appreciate who you are. If you are presented in white skin colour, be happy about yourself. If you are carefully packaged in the skin without colour, celebrate your uniqueness. The bottom line, know that you are a human being with all the potentials and abilities you need to go through life as a happy and successful person.

Success does not lie in the physicals; it is determined by two things: your mind and your character. Regardless of their externals and physicals, anybody who possesses the right mind and character can become successful. If you have these two, be positive about who you are. Know that you are a great person and carry yourself as such. Your colour, height and any other body features are all immaterial when it comes to success. Whatever your height may be, understand that it has nothing to do with your capacity to be a successful and happy person. Know that you are as good as any other person of a different height. Learn to appreciate that your greatness is in your mind and not your size or other physical features. This is why people like Mark Zuckerberg, who some people would consider short, stand tall among billionaires. Once you convince yourself and are at peace in your mind with who you are and how you look, nothing and nobody in the external world can make you feel shy about your looks.

3. Think positively about what other people think of you: Most of the time, the negative thoughts of who you are, are in your mind. Through negative imagination, you impose what you think on the people you interact with. However, one truth that you need to know is that people who matter to your success will rarely be bothered with how you look on the outside. Individuals who are material to your success will focus on what you have to offer and be least bothered about your externals. Therefore, in most cases, you are your own critic and not the external world.

If you relate to people knowing that you are a valued human being, people will see value in you and treat you with respect. However, when you interact with people with an undertone that says that you are unworthy, you will see people treat you as if you do not matter. In other words, treat yourself how you would like people to treat you, and you will see exactly that when you relate. You have the power to determine how other people treat you. If you believe that others respect and value you, that will deposit many positive thoughts in your self-esteem account. The result is that you will relate with other people and face situations with confidence. In situations where people build relational walls to block you out, know that they are the ones with a problem and not you. In such cases, be happy in your space and do not allow their walls to make you feel less valuable.

4. Think positively about outcomes: When you think negatively, you attract fear. Fear makes you think of failure and the fear to fail generates self-doubt, which manifests itself in shyness. Every action in life generates an outcome. Shyness thrives in situations where you are scared of the outcome. The possibility of failure is the primary cause of why people drawback and refrain from engaging in actions that would have propelled their success. For instance, a student who knows the answer but will not put up her hand may be scared of the following outcomes: 'If I put up my hand, other students will look at me, and I don't want that to happen. If I give a wrong answer, they will laugh at me, and I will look like a fool. My voice is not good enough. I will, therefore, not put my hand up.' This student may end up being perceived by both her teacher and classmates as being shy. However, a student with a positive attitude is likely to have such thoughts: 'I understand the subject, I will give the right answer'. Knowing that he is doing the right thing will give this student confidence. He will also know that the teacher and the students are not interested in him, but the answer. Such a positive mindset will cast out all possible fear and enable the student to confidently share his opinion.

5. Learn to love yourself: Loving yourself will liberate you from being affected by the opinions others may have on you. When you value yourself, you acquire the liberty and freedom of living your life in a world that is sterile of third-party opinion. You live your life at a higher level where only what you think of yourself matters. When your emotional life is at this level, shyness will find no room in you. When you attain such a level of emotional maturity, your mind stands at a higher level than factors that would otherwise have caused intimidation, discomfort, or self-doubt.

6. Focus on your goal: Since shyness begins in your mind, you will find it helpful to think about the goal you want to achieve every time you engage. When you condition your mind to focus on the superior purpose, you allow it to escape from the trivial. Shifting your mind from the minors will create room for your mind to focus on your engagement's core purpose. Putting your focus on the core of what you desire to achieve will make you acquire what I will call *'strategic blindness.'* This strategy will enable you to conveniently become blind to the intimidating conditions surrounding you and see only what you want to achieve.

I will give an example. We visited a church where my husband was a guest speaker. The song of meditation was provided by a young man who had a fantastic voice. He sang with passion, and you could see that he is not only singing, but he is totally lost in the world of his song. Apart from actively gesturing, he also kept his eyes shut from the beginning to the end of the song. After the church service, I congratulated his mother for having a son who could sing so well. The mother smiled with satisfaction and said, 'Listen, I realized that my son could sing when he was young. However, there was one hurdle in his way; he was very shy. He said that he could not dare stand in front of an audience and sing. Then I told him that we could find a way around that. I suggested that he closes his eyes every time he stands to sing. I told him that would help him to focus on his song and block off the people from his mind. He tried it, it worked. He has never stopped singing. His teacher at school has identified his potential, and he has started to train him to become a professional singer'. This budding superstar was manoeuvring around the shyness hurdle by focusing on his goal of becoming a singer. By continually focusing on his dream, he lost sight of the people who stood between him and his goal. By applying a simple technique of closing his eyes, he escaped from the world of shyness and attained confidence in the solitude of his mind.

Likewise, focusing on your goal will give you a practical remedy to the malady of shyness. The goal in your mind will make you unstoppable in situations where otherwise shyness would have prevailed. For example, when you have a clear goal of why you want to see the boss, you will overcome your shyness and prevail over the secretary who tries to block your way. The fact that meeting the boss is at the core of your goal, you find a way of working with the secretary to clear the way for you. On the other hand, when you have no clear sight of your goal, a stubborn secretary can easily make you give up. Suppose you are a salesperson with a target. In that case, you will not allow the mean attitude from a previous customer to make you shy from approaching other prospective clients. Constant awareness of your goal is one of the potent weapons to fight shyness as you pursue success.

7. Confront situations that make you shy: The sure way to overcome shyness is to confront situations that intimidate your mind. As said before, shyness starts in the mind and only expresses in how you react to situations. Therefore, if you want to eliminate shyness, you need to get your mind to feel comfortable in situations that trigger shyness. This means that you need to face and deal with what makes you feel shy rather than avoid it. Since shyness is closely connected to the fear emotion, you overcome shyness by facing it head-on like any other form of fear. For instance, if you are shy to speak in public, you need to train your mind to be at ease with the idea of public speaking. You can do that by altering your perception of public speaking. You can convince your mind that speaking to an audience of one thousand people is not different from talking to one person. All you do in both cases is talk. Applying the one thousand audience mindset will revolutionise how you speak by making you intentional. You will be selective in how you express yourself, the way you choose your words and how you set your intonation. Visualizing a thousand people every time you speak to one person will prepare your mind to be at ease when you face big audiences. The principle of confronting your fear applies to any situations that make you feel shy. You unlearn shyness by using every opportunity to practice confidence. As the saying goes, 'As you think, so you shall become.'

8. Dress for confidence: Confidence is an antonym for shyness. The way you dress impacts directly how you feel about yourself and how other people perceive you. Although not always the case, people can tell who you are by just a glance at your dressing. People will form their initial perception of you before you can even speak to them. How you present yourself can make people code you in their minds as either important or unimportant. The initial categorization that people assign you is likely to affect you emotionally and even impact how you behave and relate with them. When you detect a negative reception from the people you are meeting, you are likely to feel uneasy. You may feel tensed or shy to freely interact with people who categorise you as unimportant in their minds.

Although you do not derive your value from your clothes, the clothes you wear can influence how people perceive you. When you are dressed for confidence, you will feel good about yourself, and you will take your strides in a way that speaks to the rest of the world that you value who you are. Dressing per the values you stand for and the image you want to paint will oblige those around you to notice and respect you. Dressing for confidence does not mean dressing to impress others, spending a fortune or spending what you do not have. It simply means presenting yourself in a manner that makes you feel happy and comfortable to relate without feeling inadequate. It is about respecting yourself and making others comfortable to relate with you.

When you dress in a manner that boosts your image, your mind feels good, and your self-esteem gets a huge boost. When your mind is happy with the way you look, you feel ready to meet anybody and be glad to be you. There is a direct relationship between the way your dressing attracts positivity from the people you want to influence. Have you ever wondered why solicitors, bankers and CEOs have a specific code regarding how they dress? Part of it is because their business involves influencing people. This class of executives knows very well that they cannot impress people with their services unless they can relate. Appropriate dressing is among the key factor that gives executives the confidence they need to influence outcomes and prevail over situations. They know that their dressing speaks before they have the opportunity to utter a word to the client. If the dressing strategy works for top executives, it can do for you too. It will be much easier to fight shyness if the people you meet assign you the prima facie code of 'important'.

9. Invest in self-improvement: Most people who are shy will be aware of this fact. However, like many other limitations, it is not enough to just have the knowledge and awareness of the limitations. People who want to be successful do all they can to eliminate or mitigate any hurdles standing in their way to achieving. If your desire is to gain more tremendous success, you need to be intentional in confronting and overcoming shyness. You have to defy the 'once shy, always shy' attitude. Your attitude and character are not part of your DNA. This means that you can change the two and shape them in a manner that supports your success. You need to *'become'* in this aspect of your life by doing things that will enable you to replace shyness with confidence. You can do that by investing in skilling yourself up in social skill areas and any other area where you need to boost your confidence. The antidote for shyness is confidence.

Chapter two

The 'you factor' in thriving beyond hard times

Most people link their failure to hard times or crisis in their lives. Their inability to achieve is usually excused by a particular situation or circumstance they could not deal with or overcome. However, the fact is that both failures and successful people do encounter challenges. The difference is marked by the way you handle hurdles that are placed in your way to success. It is not the absence of hard times that will make you a successful person. Instead, it is the character you develop while dealing with the hard times that will determine which side of life you will fall. People who fall on the failure side of life focus on finding someone or a situation to blame for what they cannot deal with. When you focus on blaming others and justifying yourself, you cannot give attention to what you can and need to do to get out of an undesirable situation. The blame habit works against you instead of working for you. If you desire to make your situation better, spend your energy and time in a better way other than finding who to unleash your anger and frustration on.

Every crisis comes with hidden opportunities

Every crisis presents a window of opportunity. While an ordinary mind will look at predicament as the end of the road, an achieving mind will perceive hard times as the beginning of an unwritten chapter of yet another success. The attitude you develop while facing calamity and your reaction to what you meet influences how you dim or shine in a crisis. While circumstances may temporarily place you in a particular situation, your attitude and choice of response will assign your ultimate station in life.

Hard times act as a sieve, creating various categories of people; heroes and survivors, losers and winners, failures and achievers. When your path to success cannot go straight, learn the art of digging tunnels and building flyovers to reach your destination. Take a lesson from engineers. Mountains, valleys or even rivers do not stand in their way to establishing a road or rail where they desire it to be. While they cannot remove every obstacle that is in their way, they manoeuvre to get the work done. That is the spirit you need to have when dealing with hard times. You can tune your character to work for you in the same way. When facing life's valleys and mountains, your character will give you the flexibility you need to find a way out by either soaring higher than the challenge or digging deep to create an escape tunnel.

In times of crisis, victims are usually affected more by their point of focus than the crisis. To pull through a crisis and thrive, you need to make a prudent choice on where you focus and rest your mind. For example, if you get bad grades and cannot join the university, the choice you make at that point determines the extent of the impact. You can choose to give excuses to defend poor performance or can decide to make better preparation and retake the exam. If you settle for excuses, you feel the impact of the crisis for the rest of your life. However, when you choose to retake the exam, you open an alternative route to achieve even greater success. The point is, there is no single crisis without a hidden window of opportunity.

You need to discover your position of advantage in a crisis

Success does not provide immunity to calamity. There is nothing like once successful, always successful. This is why the once upon time business giants such as Sabena Airlines, Kodak, Nokia, IMB and Woolworths are now in oblivion. To remain successful, you need to possess both the capacity and flexibility that will allow you to discover your position of advantage in an emerging new situation. Unfortunately, people and institutions that never recovered from a crisis had less flexibility to fit in their new reality. To remain buoyant in your success, you must possess the capacity to re-invent your usefulness and relevancy in any situation you are pushed into by circumstances beyond your control. Rigidity in hard times may break you or hasten your expiry date.

It is not big steps that count, but small ones you take in the right direction

Success does not necessarily require big leaps. The beginning point to overcoming your crisis' is to seize every small opportunity that will take you in the right direction. You need to remain clear and focused on what you want for your life. People who manage to change their lives positively appreciate the impact of small steps in the right direction. The theory of big leaps may not work well in hard times. This is because you may spend the rest of your life waiting for that great opportunity that may never come your way. Therefore, your ability to survive and thrive in a crisis will depend on your capability to identify and implement simple but promising ideas. You do not need to have a spectacular start to achieve a grand finale.

CASE ILLUSTRATION TWO: CAPTAIN TOM MOORE

When COVID-19 hit the globe, many elderly persons felt vulnerable because the pandemic found a soft target in their age group and took advantage of their weakening health. Following the government guidelines, most senior citizens limited their areas of operation and stayed indoors.

With a few days to making one hundred years, a recent illness of skin cancer and a broken hip should have given Captain Moore enough reasons to feel vulnerable. However, while staying safe, Captain Tom Moore, a man who fought and survived World War II saw a window of opportunity to contribute to the greater cause. Perhaps, it may be true that once a soldier, always a soldier. Captain Moore refused to take the position of a spectator while the war was raging. The frontline was the medical wards, and the fight was fierce; COVID-19 versus mankind. The scourge claimed hundreds of lives each day. Many people were petrified by the furious aggression of this man-killer virus. The medics put up a good fight, and the challenge was enormous.

Although the Captain had never been engaged in disease versus man war, that was not reason enough to hold him back. His frail health and delicate age were not enough to dissuade him from pursuing a cause he believed would make a difference. His lack of medical experience could not stand in his way to being part of the team. Even though vulnerable, he refused to be on the receiving end. At nearly a hundred years of age, most people would believe that they have given the world all they had. But Captain Moore felt that he still has something more to give to his COVID-19 battered country. What many would have perceived as a liability, he turned it into his position of strength. Taking advantage of his upcoming hundredth birthday, he decided to celebrate by contributing using what he had. With the support of his walker, he accepted his family's challenge to walk one hundred laps in his garden to raise funds for NHS. Jokingly, the family initially put the fundraising target at £100, which was upgraded to a higher goal of raising £1000.

Captain Moore did not look for a spectacular way to help. Neither did he start with a grand plan. Instead, he started by using that which he had to achieve what he thought was possible. However, little did he know that by making the first step leaning on his walker for support, he had overhauled his entire life and touched an entire nation. In a few weeks, he had managed to raise £32.7 million for the NHS charities. At ninety-nine, Captain Moore held the Guinness record for the oldest person to have a UK number one when he sang 'You'll Never Walk Alone' with Michael Ball.

In less than a month, Captain Tom Moore had moved from being an oblivious retired army veteran to a national hero and achieved the Freedom of the City of London award. While he rose to the rank of a captain during his entire service in the army, his heroic spirit earned him an honorary rank of a colonel within weeks.

Very few soldiers, irrespective of rank and service, live to witness an RAF spitfire and hurricane fly-past in their honour. Colonel Moore became one of the privileged few when a spitfire and hurricane performed loops over his home in Bedfordshire on his hundredth birthday to recognise his contribution to the nation. While the colonel gave to the world by using what he had, he never anticipated that the world would give back in such generous measures. It may never have been in his wildest dreams that after a few weeks, he would be signing a £1.5 million deal to publish his life story. It may never have crossed the mind of Colonel Tom Moore that he would at the age of one hundred years old be considered by the Queen for the honour of being knighted. When you give to the world unreservedly, you attract unimaginable blessings upon yourself.

In less than two months, Captain Tom Moore managed to achieve what many people never achieve in a lifetime. He changed his title two times, moving from a captain to colonel and sir. He moved from a modest to one of the highest ranks that most people can only dream about. The image of Sir Tom Moore lit the London skies on New Year's Eve 2021. While most people of his age were engulfed in worry, Sir Moore's heroic and selfless acts sparkled the skies with hope.

Captain Tom Moore's ninety-nine years of ordinary life were overridden by one year of extraordinary achievements. His life is a clear demonstration that despite who you are and where you stand, you can still live your dream if you make the right choices and take the right actions.

On the 2nd of February 2021, Sir Tom Moore succumbed to the virus he had faithfully waged war against. The Union Jack flew on half-mast in tribute to an ordinary man who heroically touched a nation in the last year of the one hundred years of his life.

Success lessons from the life of Sir Tom Moore

While only Sir Tom Moore can live his experience, his life provides essential principles that you can apply in your journey to success.

a) You do not need the crowd to authenticate your idea: Once you feel the conviction to do something right, go ahead and start. It is your conviction and not people that will carry you through the challenging patches of life. The problem with seeking public approval is that, at best, you get mixed messages and usually overwhelming reasons why what you are contemplating is an impossibility. You can imagine the type of reaction the Colonel would have received had he sought approval for his dream of walking to raise funds for the NHS. He probably would have been overwhelmed by negative responses such as, 'you have a broken hip; there is no way you can walk that much'. Someone else would probably remind him how his recent contact with cancer makes him fall under the category of people with 'underlying conditions'. Many more would have discouraged him from venturing outside his house, cautioning that it would be a voluntary assumption of risk.

When you start something with a noble cause, the people will always join in as you move forward. Thus, a good cause advertises itself.

Since people have a high propensity to doubt, it will save

you a lot of discouragement when you skip public approval in implementing your personal plans.

b) **You are the only team you need to embark on success:** While you achieve more when you work in a team, you will find it hard to assemble a team behind you in some situations. It is easy to get people to work with you in good times, but people tend to shy away when there is a crisis. In some cases, you will not get the initial support you need, especially when you embark on what seems to most people an uphill task. In such moments, you do not have to bark off from your plan just because people are not willing to give that cheering kick-off.

When you are driven by a calling and conviction, there is nothing that you cannot achieve. A student had performed poorly in her exams, and the university could not admit her for the course she wanted. She wanted to retake the exams, but her parents withdrew their support. They thought that she should accept whatever course she was given. Rather than give up her dream, she decided to register and retake the exams. Initially, her parents were not pleased with her decision. However, when the results were out and she had scored outstanding grades, she was surprised by her parents' positive reaction. From that time onwards, they respected her choices and supported her through the rest of her education.

c) **Character is the major input you need to make a difference.** Most people will think of money, resources, or other people as the solution they need to get out of a crisis situation. However, when you have the right character, you can access all the other things you need to sort out a situation. Without the right character, it may be impossible to put to good use any other means accessible to you.

d) **Serving others produces a ripple effect.** The one kind selfless act you do for others in a time of crisis is usually reciprocated by dozens of many other benevolent acts.
In Sir Tom Moore's case, he started by offering what he had; his willingness to walk irrespective of his physical and health challenges. His act of kindness touched thousands of people worldwide who ended up raising £32.7 million. Goodness is a contagious act. At times, all you need in a crisis is a spark to light a massive fire.

e) **A crisis can be the brush you need to shine your character.**
It is possible not to know your potential until it is tested. While hard times are never desirable, they can sometimes serve the purpose of scrubbing the scales that cover who you really are. When a crisis hits, it reveals the underlying material that makes you. For some, a crisis will reveal the reality of their fake and coated personality. While to others, hard times will shine out the underlying purity and beauty of their character.
It is a crisis that turns ordinary people into heroes. Hard times can pull out your hibernating strength. While the world may have known you as an average individual, your ability to take the right actions in a crisis will allow the world to recognise you in another way. For example, for the ninety-nine years that Captain Tom Moore had been a citizen of this world, nothing spectacular was known about

him. It is the COVID-19 crisis that allowed the world to know his heroic side.

f) The number of years that you have or do not have should not inhibit your success. Someone could have whispered that your age is beyond or below what you would desire to achieve. However, the moment that you are living is the only time you are guaranteed. Therefore, use it in a manner that will take you to where you want to reach. The moment you stop achieving, you start to lose what you have.

If a ninety-nine-year-old can make a difference in an entire nation, you can also pick your to-do list and start achieving. While Sir Tom Moore provides an example of succeeding at a higher age, this is contrasted with Hazel Hill's achievement. Hazel was a thirteen-year-old schoolgirl whose contribution was fundamental in Britain winning World War II. Hazel helped resolve the contention between her father and the Generals regarding the fighter planes' design. The generals disagreed with Captain Hill's suggestion that Spitfires and Hurricanes should carry eight guns instead of four. Without another means to prove his suggestion, the Captain turned to his thirteen-year-old daughter for help. Hazel spent sleepless nights making mathematical calculations that irrefutably proved that British fighter planes needed and could carry eight guns instead of four. Her accurate calculations were accepted by the RAF and changed the Spitfire and Hurricane fighter planes' design. This helped Britain gain victory over Germany in Britain's battle and win World War II. At the age of thirteen, Hazel made a difference that resulted in Britain winning the war.

g) Only you can limit your achievements. To achieve continued success, you need to train yourself to be a perpetual achiever. However, for that to happen, your understanding of failure should change. Success becomes sweeter and sustainable when preceded by several attempts, which other people may misunderstand as failure. There is no harm in trying various ways of doing something until you find the best way to do it. However, you should guard yourself against frustration because it has silently robbed many people of their would-be success. Therefore, patience and tenacity need to be your constant ally.

Your background has no power to hold you back

Several people will wish that they were someone else. Others will wish that they were born somewhere different from where they are. It is also common to find people who wish they were from a different part of the world. Some people resent their race or caste and attribute their failures to that.

However, if you cannot achieve where you are, you will not accomplish much in a different environment. This is the reason you will have both successful and unsuccessful people from both poor and rich backgrounds. It also explains why there are outstanding people, mediocre and failures from all social classes and races. Where you come from should pose no limitation to where you want to be. While environmental and social-economic factors play a role in your journey to success or failure, your ultimate destination is sealed by the character you choose to develop along the way.

Physical, environmental, social, and economic factors can only test your tenacity to pursue success. Still, they can never stop you from achieving it. At times, your desire to light your dim corner will activate your abilities to illuminate the world. The world provides examples of men and women who, irrespective of their being born in poor families and in harsh circumstances, managed to turn themselves into what they desired to become. You do not need to have an inheritance to be able to achieve. I will use examples to illustrate this point.

CASE ILLUSTRATION THREE: HAROLD HAMM

Harold Hamm was born in what most people would agree was a poor family. With no land of their own, his parents put food on the table to feed their children from what they got out of sharecropping. Although Harold was the last of his siblings, he was not excused from contributing to his survival. He was required to do his part by helping to pick cotton from the fields.

His early exposure to work enabled him to appreciate the value of diligent work. His success is not a case of an inherited fortune, and neither is it an experience of big leaps. Harold progressively worked his way to success. The jobs that he did indicate a consistency that he knew where he wanted to reach. His previous jobs of pumping gas, repairing cars and working at the oil patch exposed him to the knowledge that was useful in his later years.

Although he started as an employee, Harold never intended to spend the rest of his life working for other people. This explains his ability to create his own company at a young age. Harold had a clear vision and possessed enough vigour to convert his dream into reality. The boy who started by picking cotton with his sharecropping parents ended up being a CEO of his own company and a billionaire. Though he began as a poor farm boy, his name stands in the Oklahoma Hall of Fame, together with names of other people of substance. It is not luck but hard work that will shape what you achieve.

No situation is too bad to jump from

CASE ILLUSTRATION FOUR: MOHED ALTRAD

The life of Mohed Altrad provides a perfect example of this truth. The case of Mohed Altrad shows that no matter how bad your situation may be, there is a way out when you have the determination. While he did not have a normal childhood, that did not deter him from becoming the person he wanted to be. Born as a result of rape, losing his mother at a tender age, and his father's rejection should have been reason enough to give him a traumatised childhood. Even though his grandmother discouraged him from going to school, thinking that he was meant to be a shepherd boy, that did not deter him from pursuing his dream. He still managed to attend school and attained excellent grades that earned him a scholarship from the Syrian government. He moved to France, where he survived on one meal a day. Despite his limitation in the French language, he completed a PhD in computer science. He became a diligent worker and saved much of his earnings which he used to buy a failing scaffolding company.

He revived the company by putting in his all. Altrad Group is a result of diligent and focused work. The company started by a once upon time penniless, orphaned, and disowned boy, employs over 39,000 people, and stands as one of the world's leading scaffolding companies. Altrad did not have to inherit a penny to become a billionaire. Each and everything he owns, he worked for it and earned it through his diligent labour.

His achievements continue to be outstanding. In 2015, Ernst and Young recognized him as the world entrepreneur of the year. While many children in his village had access to a better learning environment and better support from their parents, none rivalled his level of achievements. The bottom line is, irrespective of where you may be placed by circumstances, you can make it to where you desire to be if you dare meet the sacrifice it takes.

Hope, the one thing that you should never surrender

Diminished hope is what stops people from achieving what they desire. Hard times can make you think that what you are facing will never come to an end. You need to encourage yourself by believing that a crisis in your life does not mean the end of life. Neither do hard times mean the end of living a happy and fulfilled life. You should not allow what you are going through today to destroy your future. Your future is your unspent account; you can use it to completely overhaul your life and get where you desire to be. While a crisis may affect your present, do not give it the liberty to destroy your destiny. You may have a condition that cannot change. Know that you do not always have to change things to make life better. At times all that you need to succeed is to soar above the unchangeable. I will share with you a simple everyday illustration to explain this concept.

The air was pure and fresh as I enjoyed my walk to the gym. Suddenly, I realized that the air ahead of me was getting stuffy. The man walking in front was puffing clouds of cigarette smoke which was blown by the gentle morning breeze towards my face. I was upset by his actions, but I could not stop him from puffing his cigarette. However, I could soar above the unpleasant situation he was bringing my way. I decided to walk faster and get out of the zone that he was polluting. After taking several quick strides, I realized that his strides were bigger than mine. I changed my strategy and decided to jog. Within seconds, I was enjoying my walk again; the air was fresh.

You may not stop a crisis coming your way. However, the impact of a crisis on your life will be influenced by the choices you make. Whether you will survive or be broken by the hard times will depend on how you choose to meet your situation. In life, there will be unpleasant things that you cannot change. Things like the death of a loved one, losing a limb, losing a job, broken relationships and terminal illness, among others, are situations that may be out of your power to stop. However, while what has happened may not be changed, it is within your mandate to find a reason for living and making your life bright and meaningful. Happiness is the attitude you choose to take, even in the presence of pain.

Choosing to move on gives you the power to defy hurdles standing in your way. The secret of thriving starts with you attaining the right mindset. Before you can achieve physical and visible victory over what you are facing, you need to possess a victor's mind. You need to eliminate negative emotions within you before you can embark on success.

Be aware of self-pity, the dangerous emotion that works against you

Self-pity has never solved any problem for anybody. What

it does is make you weak, vulnerable, helpless, and chronically dependent on the mercies of other people. Self-pity destroys the potential and abilities within you to move and act. It causes you to underestimate your ability to achieve that which you desire. It numbs your power to solve problems, kills your motivation to spread your wings and fly higher and keeps you stagnant and stuck in your crisis. People who have thrived beyond their hard times are those who, despite their struggles and seemingly hopeless situations, managed to free themselves from the shackles of self-pity.

When in a crisis, turn your eyes from sympathisers and fix them on motivators. People who are willing to encourage and challenge you to pull yourself out of the situation are the right people to associate with.

Search for solutions from within you

Most of the time, people will look everywhere for answers to their problems except themselves. Perhaps, up till now, this could have been the case with you. What you need to know is that nobody will effectively and sustainably ever solve your problems. Other people may provide you with opportunities, support, and the environment you need to change your situation. However, lasting and sustainable change must come from you. For instance, you may look at your husband, your wife, your parents, your fiancé, your friends, your boyfriend, your girlfriend, your children, your neighbour, church members, your pastor, your manager, your boss and your workmates, among others. However, none of them will sustainably change your situation if you do not take responsibility and be the pivot of the change you want to see in your life. While it is okay to seek support when you need it, it is wrong to think that another person is responsible for fixing problems in your life.

While people will cause a lot of mess in your life, you stand a better chance of coming out of it if you pick the broom and sweep the mess out. You should never wait for others to come and fix your problems because people who mess you up will continue to enjoy their lives as if nothing ever happened. Therefore, if you do not sweep that mess out, you and not them will continue living with it. For instance, while it hurts so bad for your husband to leave you for another woman or your wife to leave you for another man, it is self-destroying to put your life to a halt if your spouse divorces you. While it is good to do everything possible to win your spouse back and save your marriage, if you see that the other party is resolved to never come back, you need to put closure on the chapter and find new meaning for your life. Get a cause to live for and a reason to be happy. You need to stop punishing yourself for someone who has decisively left you. He or she is not worth it because your hurt feelings will not be noticed let alone be appreciated. While it is true that people get you into a bad situation, only you are responsible for getting yourself out.

The danger of perceiving other people as a solution to your problems

When you consider people to be a solution to what you are going through, you will want to change them to fit the type of solution you have in your mind. For instance, if you are going through hard time because you are a single woman, you may find yourself wanting to change every single eligible man you meet to become your boyfriend, fiancé, or husband. Therefore, your motivation for relating will be influenced by the objective of what you want the person to be to you. When you behave like that, you are likely to scare people from wanting to relate with you because they perceive you as being aggressive, desperate, or pushy in the relationship. As a result, instead of attracting relationships, you end up repelling them.

You have the ability not only to survive but to thrive

Your ability to survive and thrive beyond a crisis does not depend on restoring your situation to what it was before the crisis. Some things cannot be restored, and some cases are irreversible. To succeed in your new condition, you need to stop focusing on changing other people and changing circumstances and focus on adapting yourself. The point is, some people cannot be changed, and some conditions cannot be changed either. Therefore, the time and efforts that you put into changing the unchangeable get wasted. On the other hand, the power to change you entirely lies in your hands.

When you change you, it gives you the edge to relate with that which cannot be changed. When you choose to shift your eyes from looking at someone else and focus on what you can do, you will be amazed by the progress and eventual success you achieve. People get frustrated in achieving the change they desire to see because they focus on changing others. Those who concentrate on changing others are often blind to their own follies. They tend to push other people to become what they want them to be. In short, they demand that someone else makes the move while they remain in their comfort. This is the reason you will hear statements like:

'David needs to change the way he behaves; otherwise, I am

done with this relationship.'

People who behave like that find it hard to take responsibility and may never see the need to make themselves better persons. Individuals with such a mindset always think that they are correct and someone else is wrong. Possessing such a mindset is a hindrance that will stand in your way to make your life better because you think that someone else is responsible for your failures. Never at any point will you look at how you could have caused or contributed to your situation. To move out of your crisis, you need to push yourself. I will give an example.

The 14th of June 2017 was a fateful night when the twenty-four-story Grenfell Tower went ablaze, registering one of the worst modern disasters in London that claimed seventy-two lives. During a TV interview, one of the survivors of this unfortunate disaster indicated that she was unhappy with how those in authority handled the situation. She pointed out that she needed counselling services, and nobody had bothered to give her the service that she very much needed. When asked if she had made any efforts to approach organisations that were known to provide counselling services to the members of her community, this was her response:

'Why should we go to them when we are the victims? They are the ones who are supposed to come to us.'

While it was sad for the lady to undergo such a horrible disaster, the fact that she seemed to be stuck in it was more disturbing. She lacked the will to take any initiative to make her situation better. In her perspective, she was the victim, and because of that, she needed other people to fix everything in her life, including the things that she could do. When you are in a crisis, you have a choice; you can decide to sit and wait for others to sort you out, or you can use the remaining efforts you have to push yourself out of the crisis.

Related to the same Grenfell disaster, the reporter interviewed Ines Alves, a sixteen-year-old teenage girl who escaped the fire on the same fateful night. That night, Ines' father came to her room and asked her to get ready to leave the flat because the building was on fire. The teenager said that the only thing she grabbed from her room as she escaped was the chemistry notes she had been revising that night. When asked why she did that, the teenager said she thought she would use the time of waiting to revise her notes. In the morning, while the deadly flames were devouring and destroying what had been her home, she walked away, leaving behind the ruins. She went to school and sat for her GCSE chemistry exam in the same clothes she had escaped. When she got her results, she had scored an 'A' in the paper she did as her home was burning to ashes. That is what made her a news item. She made a brave choice to thrive above her disaster. She could not stop the fire, but she chose not to allow it to destroy her future.

In this example, we have two people facing the same crisis. The marked difference is in the character they exhibit while responding to the disaster. The difference in their mindset eventually determined how they faced and lived their lives during and after the crisis. The point is, there is no disaster big enough to hold you back. You can only be held back if you do not know what you want. Irrespective of how bad your crisis is, there is something that you can do. The teenage girl lost all her family belongings in the fire. The only thing she escaped with was her chemistry notes, and she made good use of that. Whatever little you are left with, put that tiny thing to the best use. You do not need to have significant opportunities to pick up your life. Even if it is only a thread left, hook your life on it rather than let go.

Take time to build your success

Steve Thomson and his wife Lenka were in November 2019 revealed as the winners of the £105 million EuroMillions jackpot. Such quick success sounds sweet and appealing to many people. It is a cherished fantasy of many to go to sleep as paupers and wake up the following day as millionaires. However, if that is your route to achieving success, you have higher chances of going to your grave still waiting for your dream. If you want success, you have to build it. Constructing success involves approaching it, one step at a time.

People that resign from pursuing success do so because they want it instant. Seeking success is like building a house. It takes time, resources, and requires a plan. It is your plan that informs how your house will look once constructed. Therefore, your first step to succeeding is to plan for your life and establish standards, goals and milestones that will enable you to achieve. Attach time as a way of monitoring your progress. Although time is a constant resource given to every person in equal measure, the way it is used determines achievers and losers.

Your mind

Every system must have a central command point where the purpose and the functions of the establishment are centrally managed, monitored and coordinated. To position yourself in the success mode, you need to perceive your body as a system and your mind as the command and control centre. Your mind plays the role of aligning the activities you engage in to fit your calling and purpose. If you want to achieve outstandingly, you need to relate with your mind to support your calling and purpose. Your mind is the most potent weapon that you will ever have. It can make or destroy you.

The mind can be categorised as either static or progressive based on the owner's choices and attitudes. However, irrespective of the above categorisation, every mind can grow or degenerate. What makes your mind defined as static or progressive is determined by what you feed it on and how you choose to engage it. A mind fed with the right thoughts, exposed to appropriate material, and progressively engaged will grow into a progressive mind. And likewise, a mind that feeds on garbage, kept idle, not stretched, sheltered from challenges, and not actively engaged will degenerate into a static mind. A progressive mind will see potentials, possibilities, and opportunities in all circumstances. In contrast, a static mind will see and settle on the negatives and impossibilities in every situation.

While the human embryo starts to develop its brain in the third week after conception, it is believed that the human baby is born with an empty mind. Scholars use the analogy of computer hardware and software to describe the relationship between the brain and the mind. The way the software is programmed into the computer determines its performance, so does your mind affect your brain's performance.

From the time you were born, what you were exposed to informed the mind you developed. As you grow older, your choices, actions and environment continue to form your mind. Therefore, the mind that you currently have is created by parenting, environment, and choices. The fact that a human being is born with an empty mind is good news. This is because while the brain is predetermined to a significant extent, it is entirely within your power to determine your mind. The two substantial factors in determining the mind are parenting and the choices of the individual. It is also true that the environment one is exposed to has an impact on the mind. However, this type of impact is not absolute. While the environment can affect your mind, your mind can also override your environment's negative influence.

There are examples of children who grew up amidst a grossly corrupting environment, and their minds remained unaffected. A good case is the story of the boy Samuel found in the Bible in Samuel chapters one to three. Samuel was the son of Hannah. According to the promise Samuel's mother had made to the Lord, she took her son to the temple after weaning him. At this stage, he was young and vulnerable. Samuel was to live with the family of Eli, the priest. Eli's house and the entire temple surroundings were toxic because of Eli's sons' evil doings. Eli's boys practised every bad habit of the time, and evil-doing was their pleasure. However, young Samuel remained as pure as a lily growing in muddy waters. The toxic environment that he was placed in could not contaminate his mind. This was because of the values imparted by his mother and the personal choices he made.

Even in cases where your parents exposed you to harmful and damaging influence, you can still overcome that. You always have a choice to rewrite your mind. The life of King Josiah is a good case. You can read the entire life of King Josiah in the Bible in the book of 2 Chronicles, chapters 33 and 34. King Josiah was a descendant of evil-doing kings. His grandfather

King Manasseh had practised all sorts of evil, and his father, King Amon, outdid King Manasseh in wickedness. However, when his father was assassinated, Josiah became king at the age of eight and made decisions that gave him the mind that he needed to become a successful ruler of his people.

The point is, while you may not choose how your parents influenced your mind, that cannot stop you from succeeding. This is because your mind is a flexible re-writable software. You can change and reprogramme how your mind functions. Again, I will use an example from the world of computers to explain how you can achieve the mind you desire and the mind that will work for you. Before the current internet dominated era, data used to be processed, shared and stored in very different ways from what we have today. In 1997, the Compact Disc-Rewritable (CD-RW) was introduced. The CD-RW made it possible to rewrite new data on top of the existing information. By so doing, the previously existing data would be erased. This can, to some extent, compare to how your mind works. While you may not reverse your past, you can re-write over it and create the new mind that works for you. By developing a fresh mind, the old mind will be erased by default.

This implies that you have the power to develop an achieving mind irrespective of your stage and station in life. Therefore, instead of wasting the remaining time blaming your parents, other people or circumstances, focus on re-writing your mind. You need a new mindset if you want to achieve exceptionally.

In her work, *Mindset, The New Psychology of Success,* Professor Carol Dweck categorises the mindset into *fixed* and *growth* mindsets. She explains that each person has either or the other of the two mindsets. She demonstrates that the type of mindset one has is not stagnant and can be changed at any time. She underscores the fact that mindset affects the level of achievement. The great thing about the mind is that it is not limited by skin colour, background, physical abilities or station in life. Interestingly, while you may not choose your race or skin colour, you have the mandate to select the type of mind you want to be associated with.

When you embark on the journey to success, you must start with the right mind and keep an eye on it. This is because while your brain has unlimited potential to function, its performance level can be curtailed by the state of mind you assign yourself. While your brain is technically the control room for your entire body system, your mind can control and influence its functioning. Comparably the brain and the mind are like the head and the neck analogy. While the brain is the chief, the mind can turn the brain in the direction it wants. Therefore, your brain's size, shape, and quality may not mean much if you do not apply the right mindset. Your mind determines and controls the functioning of your brain. When you have a positive mind, it will be a valuable tool in enabling you to overlook the unpleasant process you have to go through on your way to success. You have the prerogative of choosing the type of mind you want to partner with. A positive mind will be your ally in keeping you focused and restraining you from quitting.

Your mind is your closest partner in achieving success. You need to stress-proof it and take good care of it so that it can take good care of your success. Again, using the example of a computer, a computer that is overloaded gets slow and can be frustrating to work with. You need to keep a clear and clean mind so that it has room to accommodate the positive things that contribute to your success. Do not load it with things that will hinder its functioning. Things like revenge, hatred, unforgiveness, envy, malice, alcohol, drugs, smoking, violence, and pornography are examples of elements that can clog and incapacitate your mind from optimum functioning. A clear mind has a better capacity to be efficient, think, plan, reason, solve problems and make prudent decisions. It benefits you and enhances your success when you keep a clear and focused mind.

'Finally, brethren, whatever things are true, whatever things are noble, whatever things are just, whatever things are pure, whatever things are lovely, whatever things are of good report, if there is any virtue and if there is anything praiseworthy, meditate on these things.' [12]

When you practice the habit of having a positive mind, you will realize the good hidden in every situation. No matter how bad the experience may seem to be, you can find a reason to be optimistic.

Your mind can alter the functioning of your body. This makes your mind a powerful tool you can use to your advantage. Unknown to many is that a powerful and positive mind has more capacity to fight disease than the most potent medicine taken with a pessimistic or fatalistic mind. I am not saying that you should not go to the doctor or not take your medication. You need to see your GP when you are not well and take your medicine. What I am bringing to your attention is the power within your mind. I will give an example:

My sister-in-law was diagnosed with type 2 diabetes. Before the doctors started her on medication, she made up her mind to reverse the disease. She followed the health practices and the diet recommended by a lifestyle doctor. She had to let go of many things that she loved eating, drinking and doing. By engaging the power of her mind, she started learning to eat, drink and do the things that she previously did not like that much. She overhauled her entire lifestyle. After three months, she went for another test. The results indicated that her condition had changed from having diabetes to prediabetes. My sister-in-law was thrilled with the results. In just three months, she reversed her diabetes to prediabetes because she determined to claim her life back.

In another case, a friend of mine used her mind to alter her baby's birth. My friend's son was due in the first week of September. She, however, desperately wanted her baby born before the end of August so that he did not miss the cut-off date for the beginning of the school academic year. My friend used her mind to make it happen. One morning she decided that she was going to have the baby that day. She started telling her mind that she was going into labour and that the baby was on his way. Although that was not happening, she altered her mind by creating her own reality. She went on with doing the final packing for her hospital bag and took it in the car. She came back to the house and believed that she was having contractions. She started to behave as if she was in labour. A few hours later, the actual labour pains began and increasingly intensified. She was rushed to hospital and had her baby born at the very end of August. That is the power of the mind.

Your mind can alter life reality and create its own. You can use your mind as an accessible tool to find a way through challenging situations as you advance in your success.

The effect of your mental wellbeing on the capacity to achieve

It is vital to keep conscious of the fact that the functioning of your brain can be affected by the state of your mental health. Therefore, you must become intentional in taking care of your mental health the same way you do for your physical health.

You need good mental health to generate constructive ideas, achieve success and put your success to good use. Mental health is a term that is gaining a central place in our times. However, it remains relatively new when recognizing its importance in attaining, retaining, and enjoying success. There is a need to comprehend the link between your mental health and your ability to achieve.

Mental health has been defined by the World Health Organization as:

'A state of mental wellbeing in which every individual realizes his or her own potential, can cope with the normal stresses of life, can work productively and fruitfully and is able to make a contribution to her or his community.' [13]

Although you may have heard this definition several times, it is worth throwing more light to illuminate how the embedded principles affect your ability and level of achievement. The World Health Organization definition presents four pillars that directly link mental health to attaining success. We shall take a look at each of these pillars.

a) **Ability to realize your potential:** When you have good mental health, you gain the capacity to discover your unique skills. Each person is created with abilities to achieve in a unique way from the rest of the world.

Your inability to succeed is not a lack of potential but your limitation to dig deep into the wealth mines within you. You do not access success from the world; success is in-built in you; you just have to know how to effectively deliver it. It is your ability to share it with the world that will make you stand out. When you know your unique abilities, you can change the world by sharing what only you can give.

While everyone is gifted, potential is unique to individuals. The inability to associate with your own aptitudes and imitating other people's abilities will hinder you from attaining outstanding success. While it is good to be inspired, it is self-undermining to imitate another person. You can never be him or her because you are endowed uniquely. Your beginning point to attaining unrivalled success is to know your uniqueness.

b) **Coping with stresses of life:** Stress is not bad when you know how to relate to it. In fact, it can even play a valuable role in driving you to achieve. However, long term stress and lack of capacity to handle it can be detrimental to your health and limit your capacity to function. Your mental well-being is tested by your ability to cope and still remain productive in stressful situations. Life is littered with patches of stress. These tend to be more prominent when you are on your way to attaining success. It is impossible to achieve and sustain success if you cannot contain and thrive alongside stress.

Many people do give up their efforts to succeed because they fail to navigate their way through stress to reach where they want to be. Several people fail to achieve not because they do not know what to do but rather because they cannot be bothered or take it anymore. To avoid being one of the deserters who start and abandon projects, you need to be intentional in stress-proofing your mental health. Stress-proofing your mental health does not mean that you eliminate stressful situations. Instead, it means that your mind will be better equipped to handle stress without being negatively affected or cracked by it. Stress-proofing your mind is a daily and continuous activity. The steps are straightforward, but most people ignore them, and they end up paying an enormous price. Habits like being proactive, avoiding procrastination, positive thinking, active relationship with God, eating well, sunshine, fresh air, exercising, temperance, rest, forgiveness, positive relationships, and avoiding drugs and alcohol use are all things that can be done. However, many ignore these simple remedies of common sense and lose a lifetime of hard work.

c) **Your productivity level:** Good mental health will enable you to engage in productive work and make your work fruitful. To achieve success, you need to know and manipulate the principle of the multiplier effect. Good mental health will give you the capacity to identify and engage in projects that have bounty outputs. It is hard to attain outstanding success if you invest your energy and resources in ventures that yield little and keep you at survival.

Good mental health will give your mind the sharpness it needs to generate productive and fruitful ideas. While productive may be limited in the number of cycles, fruitful implies perpetual increase. In other words, success continues to beget more success. Such a level of planning and execution requires the existence of sound and dependable mental health. While it is practical to encounter failure, you may never attain success unless you bother to establish why things did not work out previously. Unfortunately, while it is common for people to point out why they did not succeed, rarely do people look at themselves as a possible cause for their failure.

It is possible to repeatedly fail because your mind is not prepared to engage and support you in what you are doing. When you start a project with poor mental health, your mind may remain disengaged. The implications of this are that you are likely to make bad decisions and disastrous judgements of the situations that affect your success. If you find yourself engaging in projects that never yield results, it could be a good idea to check if there is a gap between what you are doing and your state of mind. When you embark on creating success, you need your entire mind to throw its weight into what you are doing. You need focus; you need attention. You cannot do that unless your mind is entirely directed to where you are heading.

d) Contributing to your life as an individual and to the lives of others: Good mental health makes your success positively change your life and positively affects those around you. Your mental health status would be questioned if your success did not add value to your life and the lives of others. Success ceases to make meaning when it becomes an end in itself. You achieve more when you change lives than when you amass physical possessions. People who have got the best satisfaction from their success are those who used it to change the world even though their direct actions impacted just one life. The ripple effect of positive influence can be massive. The life of one individual that you positively change can make a difference in millions of lives.

The impact of forgiveness on your success

While forgiveness is an act that can be achieved by decision and choice, it also has an emotional aspect that affects the state of your mental and physical health. Your attitude to forgiveness will bear implications on your overall performance as a person. Many people tend to limit forgiveness to be a religious obligation.

'For if you forgive men their trespasses, your heavenly Father will also forgive you. But if you do not forgive men their trespasses, neither will your Father forgive your trespasses.' [14]

Forgiveness goes much far beyond the above religious injunction because it affects the spiritual, emotional and physical aspects of life. The capacity to offer forgiveness links one's emotional health and the quality of mind. People who practice genuine forgiveness are likely to enjoy better emotional health and relate better with others. When you have bad emotional health, it can stand in the way you connect with business partners. Also, bad emotional health is likely to make you behave in a manner that will repel people from supporting you.

When you work with people, they are prone to offend you, and you are likely to hurt them. The remedy to keep a friendly work environment and avoid losing valuable team members is to practice the virtue of forgiving. You earn higher respect when you ask the people you lead to forgive you when you offend them or are wrong.

The other dimension of forgiveness that is equally important is the ability to forgive yourself. At times you will make silly mistakes that are fatal to your enterprise, and you will find that some of those mistakes may be irreversible. However, even in such cases, you need to be able to forgive yourself. When you deny yourself forgiveness, you hold yourself back from moving forward or starting all over again. Lack of self-forgiveness activates regret, which is one of the negative emotions that push you into reverse gear. You begin to accelerate backwards instead of moving forward. When you struggle to forgive yourself, you may never be able to forgive other people.

A resourceful employee is much more important than a few thousand-pounds loss he may cause you due to a genuine error. A mistake that results in valuable lessons converts into an asset. Therefore, forgiveness is not only good for your spiritual health but also vital for your success.

Encourage yourself as often as possible

Discouragement is the number one enemy of success. No matter how far you may have climbed the tower of success, despair has the potential to pull you down. A few moments lingered in the domain of discouragement can push you to the bottom irrespective of achievement level. If you want to maintain and gain more altitude in success, you must avoid running on people's kudos and thumbs-up. Controllers know how to use their thumbs and words in a manner that puts you where they want you. Encouragement from other people is capricious. There are moments when those who sung praises for you yesterday will be ready to stone you today. The life of King David in the Bible provides an example of this. Although David was a mighty warrior, he at some point experienced the wrath of his men, who were prepared to get rid of him in one moment.

Success does not put you out of reach of negative people. Success does not shield you from unfair blame or attacks. When you feel that you are unfairly treated, you must encourage yourself to keep going.

'And David was greatly distressed for the people spoke of stoning him because the soul of all the people was grieved, every man for his sons and for his daughters: but David encouraged himself in the Lord his God.' [15]

David had been a man of perpetual success. However, because of one incident not linked to his weakness as a warrior and leader, his men were ready to stone him and get rid of him. That is the nature of people. They will treat you as disposable when they feel disappointed in their areas of interest; they will want to put you away.

Achieving success does not necessarily insulate you from people's criticisms, attacks, and blame. People will find something to blame you for, irrespective of how much you have and are still achieving. Therefore, take both people's praises and criticism in the same way; they are both immaterial in your journey to success. You need neither to become a successful person.

The critical thing you need to do in your hilltop and valley moments is to focus on your dream. To achieve continued success, you need to create a well of encouragement within your heart. Learn to thrive without people's validation. Having God's approval and caring for humanity is what counts in your journey to success.

Refuse to carry other people's fears

The fear emotion helps keep you safe. However, your body is designed to experience and positively utilize only appropriate amounts of this emotion. Subjecting your body to carrying fear from other people results in an overdose and burdens your system, which can lead to *performance paralysis*. When you accept to bear other people's fear, you will not be able to do things you have the capacity to do. Embracing fear from other people significantly reduces your safe area of operation. Fear makes you less adventurous, less innovative, and probably never creative. All these are counterproductive in your journey to success.

You cannot succeed unless you give yourself the freedom to try different things and take logical risks. When you give other people permission to load you with their fear burdens, you allow them to control your life. Controllers will know which fear button to press to keep you where they want you. You will find it complicated to stay on the course of success if you do not have the freedom to control your own emotions. This is because the nature of your feelings will impact the choices and decisions that you make. Getting in charge of your fear emotion will give you the confidence and conviction you need to make life-changing decisions.

People that fail are held back by fear, while those that succeed are driven by faith. You cannot experience good emotional health when you allow other people's emotions to dictate how you feel. Adopting other people's fear can cause you anxiety and increase your stress levels. While fear does not solve problems, it can significantly block finding logical interventions to situations. Being empathetic does not mean that you share someone's fears. Fear from other people will put you out of control and cause you to do things you are not supposed to do.

An excellent example of this is the toilet paper panic in Britain during the 2020 COVID-19 pandemic first lockdown. While one could explain the rationality for stocking food, the panic and hoarding of toilet paper rolls remain astounding. While toilet-roll is essential, it is not one of the items you would expect to be in shortage in a first world country. Pandemic or no pandemic, it would be ridiculous to doubt the capacity of one of the world's super economies to maintain a stable supply of toilet papers to its population. However, the unprecedented purchase of toilet paper rolls during Britain's first COVID-19 pandemic lockdown left shelves in almost all stores, big and small, stripped of every single toilet roll. No matter how often the shelves were re-stocked, people did not allow this product to stay on the shelf. The limitation on the number of toilet papers one could buy did not help either. The constant reminders played in stores, reminding shoppers that they did not need to buy more than they need, did not stop the rush for toilet paper rolls.

While it went that far, the interesting question is, how did it all start? How did people who live in the sixth-largest economy on the globe doubt their country's capacity to supply enough toilet paper rolls? It all boils down to fear. Perhaps, a few shoppers who feared running out of toilet paper during the lockdown decided to fill their shopping trolleys with the product. Maybe, when other shoppers saw this, they feared that toilet rolls were getting scarce, and they too decided to stock the item, just in case. This fear was shared between friends, households, and colleagues. Within a short time, the entire country shared the fear, and there was a 'toilet roll rush.' Soon people were driving for miles in the hunt for toilet rolls. What could have started as a few people's fear soon turned into a national panic. The national rush for toilet paper rolls in Britain in the 21st-century is a perfect example of how fear can impair common sense and alter good judgement. In this case, the fear of a few individuals created a problem where there should not have been any.

If you want to beat fear at its own game, you must approach the unknown with calmness and confidence. When you come to know the unknown, you will realize that most human fears are misconceptions. There is a substantial variation between the Britain 2020 COVID-19 national lockdown with the Britain 2021 COVID-19 nationwide lockdown. While the lockdown circumstances remained pretty much similar, the 2021 lockdown did not cause panic buying. Shelves in stores remained fully stocked for all items that were hoarded during the 2020 national lockdown. The difference is, the 2020 lockdown was the unknown, while the 2021 lockdown was the known. People knew what to expect during the 2021 lockdown. They know that there will be enough for everyone, so there was no point hoarding.

Fear is highly contagious and can be as destructive as a plague. Therefore, keep away from it and do not allow anyone to impose on you this unnecessary burden. At times, people will want to stop you from achieving what they have failed to accomplish by planting the seeds of fear and doubt in your mind. For example, it is possible to give up on having a relationship with God because another person planted seeds of fear in you about God. People who want to ignite fear in you will start by blowing up your inadequacies, shortcomings, and failures. Then, they will want you to believe that you are too bad to be accepted. The fear not to meet expectations can cause you to distance yourself from God and shun other good relationships.

Fear stops you from trying things and gaining personal experience. Fear can cause you to live your life based on what others think or what they have gone through. Such fear robs your identity and steals your potential to become who you were created to be. For instance, someone may have misled your understanding of who God is. They may have used their own fears to influence your opinion about God. However, when you refuse to share someone else's fear about God and decide to establish your own relationship with Him, you will be surprised. You will discover that contrary to what you were meant to believe, God has always loved you.

'But God demonstrates His own love toward us, in that while we were still sinners, Christ died for us.' [16]

Many people that do not succeed fail because they feared to fail

I will use an example from our children to illustrate this. Ariella, our old daughter, sings well. Netanella, our second daughter, refused to sing because she was afraid that she could not sing as good as her sister. We knew that unless she overcame her fear of not singing like Ariella, she would never be able to sing. Our strategy to get her to start singing was to make her believe in singing like 'Netanella'. Our challenge was to guide her into producing the Netanella brand and not an imitation of her sister.

Once she realized that she needed to work on being herself and not converting into another Ariella, her fear disappeared. Self-doubt was replaced with confidence, and she was ready to experience her own success. Soon she was singing duets with Ariella. She was comfortable with high notes and was enjoying the experience. She is now working towards recording her solos. Fear has the power to hold you back from achieving and make you live your life in constant comparison. When you make yourself a victim of comparison, your identity gets eroded. Therefore, avoid losing yourself by refraining from playing the comparison game. The danger of this game makes you live your life as an imitation of something you are not. If you want to attain tremendous success, you need to first find yourself and be comfortable pursuing and achieving success in your own way.

Invest in hope

Hope is fundamentally different from wishful thinking. While wishful thinking is dormant, hope is perpetually active. The more hope units you deposit into your mind, the more tenacious your willpower will get. Hope is a crucial ingredient in dealing with the hurdles you will undoubtedly encounter on your route to success. There will be times when your output is far less than your input. Moments when you feel like you are dealing with constant challenges, and the most appealing alternative is to give it all up.

Discouragers will be positioned at every stage on your way to success. Such people will delight in highlighting your failures and deflating your achievements. They will relish pointing out the impossibilities in your plans. Many will mercilessly punch holes in every idea you present. Others will get their satisfaction by trying to pull you down and rejoice when things are not going your way. The presence of such people requires you to keep your hope levels at the optimum. It is the unbeatable power of hope that will enable you to carry on when everyone seems to be against you, and you stand in the valley of success. It is hope that will move you to achieve even when no single person believes in you.

When you have hope, it will enable you to do the manageable while you plan to move mountains that stand in your way. Hope will make it possible to break mountains in your way into anthills and deal with each, one at a time. Optimism will push you to take hope steps and engage in hope actions. It is the refusal to give up hope that turns ordinary people into inventors, heroes, and social champions. For example, hope kept Thomas Edison focused when he failed one thousand times before he successfully invented the light bulb. In his mind, he saw the one thousand times he had to try as steps to success. While wishful thinking is building castles in the air, hope is building your castle, one stone at a time.

The price of success

There is a price to everything that has value. Even in situations where something may appear free, a fee has been paid by someone, and you are privileged to enjoy their generosity.

For example, while we are often told that salvation is free, this is not true because salvation was purchased at a priceless cost which is the life of the Son of God. No price could be higher than that. When we know the value of our salvation, we learn to appreciate what God did for us.

'For God so loved the world that He gave His only Son, that whoever believes in Him shall not perish but have eternal life.' [17]

This makes salvation a priceless gift; the cost is matchless.

Many people want success, but a few are ready and committed to paying what it takes to succeed. You need more than a dream to acquire success. There is a broad misconception about what it takes to become successful. For instance, many people think that you need money to achieve. However, access to cash, resources, and wealth does not necessarily make you a successful person. It is possible to inherit wealth and still live and die poor.

The difference between achievers and non-achievers is the willingness to pay the price of success. The cost of success is immeasurable. Yet, it is everything you do to push yourself to be the best version that you can ever be.

The currency you use to buy success

(i) Time

Time is a constant resource that is given to every person in equal quantities. Every human being has access to twenty-four hours and seven days a week.

The wealthiest person in the world has the same amount of

time as the poorest person in the world. The fundamental difference between the two people is how they use their time. While a person who wants to achieve will seek to put each second of his time to productive use, a person who will fail will not have a smart plan to effectively use his time. While achievers seek to save time and invest it, losers look for ways to spend time because they think they have too much of it. One of the amber signs that will signal to you that you are on the road to failure will be the tendency of feeling bored. Boredom is an indicator to tell you that you are not investing your time. It is frequently said that time is a resource. Unfortunately, few people comprehend and appreciate the meaning and reality embedded in that statement. When you start to perceive time as a useful resource, you will stop wasting it and start investing it. Many people who ended up poor never realized the value of time and thus never invested it to yield the most returns. Achievers do not look at time as a consumable; they perceive it as an investable asset.

The day you start school, you begin to invest or spend your time. That has a significant contribution to who you end up as an adult. It is possible to look at one's time chart and predict the outcome. You can predict what a child who spends his time on a play station, TV and phone will become. Likewise, it does not need a specialist to predict the future of a child who invests his time in useful activities. While failures invest in temporary pleasurable activities, achievers invest in long-term life-changing engagements.

The cost that you have to pay to achieve is the discomfort involved in making the right choices.

(ii) Self-discipline

It is impossible to achieve without having discipline. It is the self-discipline that will keep you on course and protect you from being distracted. Self-discipline will enable you to exercise self-control in situations where you are facing competing interests. For example, while a self-disciplined student may feel the desire and urge to watch a favourite TV soap, he will exercise self-control. Without self-discipline, a student will live her life according to the whims of the moment. For instance, it will not matter if she has a test the next day; she will still find no problem spending the evening in front of the TV because that is what she enjoys doing. Self-discipline will help you to resolve the conflict between interests and priorities.

(iii) Hard work

To achieve, you need to work hard. There is no magic pill to attaining success. Success is a by-product of persistent, diligent hard work. The consideration payable for success is hard work. No work yields failure. If you desire God's blessings, you have a duty to work hard and present to Him something that He will bless. It is not only unpractical, but it is also ridiculous to choose idleness and ask God for blessings.

'In all labour, there is profit, but idle chatter leads only to poverty.' [18]

God's blessings are activated by diligent labour.

'Whatever you do, work at it with all your heart as working for the Lord, not for men.' [19]

Therefore, stop dreaming about success and focus on making your success happen.

'He who works his land will have abundant food, but the one who chases fantasies will have his fill of poverty.' [20]

People that achieve make a choice to work hard irrespective of the challenges involved. It is dishonourable to give up a project just because it is stretching your abilities. If you want to grow into something outstanding, you have to learn to cope with the stretching pains that come with engaging in a rewarding project. Many people saw their dreams go under the bridge because when the going got tough, they lacked the stamina to keep going and opted for the easy alternatives. They settled for something less challenging but also less rewarding.

A typical example of this is students who start with high goals. However, as the studies begin to get more complex, challenging, and demanding, they prefer the less challenging path and lower their bar for achieving. Eventually, they swing from one course to another and end up settling for something less rewarding. As they step into their zone of comfort, they end up settling for the cheapest. The same goes for a career. Most people will tend to accept that which is less engaging rather than pursue a challenging profession. However, at times choosing the easy option also implies embracing a life of mediocrity.

Working hard does not mean spending your entire time doing the job. Fruitful work involves the art of identifying your goals, making your priorities, and investing your time where you will achieve maximum profitable and sustainable outputs. Productive hard work is achieved by working SMART (Specific- Manageable- Activities -Rateable -Timebound). If you desire to see your work's outcome, you need to ensure that the task you engage in is *specific*. You are likely to achieve disappointment when you invest in something that you cannot clearly define. Your business or work needs to have a clear identity regarding what you want to do and aim to achieve. You get discouraged when you engage in a project that is not *manageable*. It is crucial to know that you can handle the project before getting engaged in it. People fail to achieve if they cannot identify *activities* that will drive their project to success. When you start a project without separating activities that drive and deliver success from time-wasting and resource-consuming activities, you become disillusioned. Success becomes real when it is *rateable*. If you desire to achieve, you must establish a mechanism for rating your progress from the start to completing any engagement. Projects that are not *timebound* have the potential to become stale and out of touch with their relevancy. They can also be profoundly demotivating and consume tremendous resources without giving any results. It is rewarding if, at the end of the day, end of a season, end of a phase, you can look back and put your hands on what you have achieved.

(iv) Supportive relationships

You need to build and maintain a vertical relationship with God. This is because you cannot attain satisfying success without having an active and meaningful connection with God. You need the wisdom to achieve, and as it stands, God is the source of true wisdom.

'The fear of the Lord is the beginning of wisdom, and the knowledge of the Holy One is understanding.' [21]

To attain meaningful success, it will require that you invest some of your time in horizontal relationships with your family, friends, workmates, and the community. It is a colossal mistake to sacrifice human relations on the altar of success. We all know of the saying that 'no man is an island'. You need active people in your life who will give you a sense of belonging. You need people you can go to and offload the stress you accumulate at work. You need people who will share your goals, celebrate your success and support you when facing challenges. In short, you need people to enjoy your success.

People who get wealthy but have lives devoid of meaningful intimate human relationships live in isolation, imprisoned by their success.

Wealth can never fill the gap created by social isolation. It is the attempt to fill the inner void that has seen wealthy men and women lose their lives to drugs. Unfortunately, tranquillizers can never take the place of human relations in terms of giving comfort, support, appreciation, and a sense of belonging.

(v) Integrity

Integrity is a virtue that is getting scarce in 21st Century communities. However, to those that still seek it and hold to it, it becomes an invaluable asset. Success presupposes engagement in some business relationships with other parties. Your level of integrity will determine your dependability. Integrity is a valuable asset that places you in a position of advantage over your competitors who do not have it. This could be the only advantage that you have over others and why you are preferred over thousands providing the same service. I will give a short illustration.

With the online market becoming more popular because of its convenience, my husband and I, at times, do our shopping online. Every time we visit online shops, my husband prefers that we purchase items from Amazon. Irrespective that the same items may be offered at a lower price by other online shops. His reason for choosing Amazon over others is the level of trust. My husband trusts Amazon to keep his personal data safe and believes it will deliver the purchased items. I believe there are millions of other people worldwide who are convinced about Amazon's integrity. That could be a substantial contributing factor for Amazon taking the lion's share of the online retail market. Several companies do not realize that they can continue to ride high only when they maintain integrity. No matter how huge a company may be, it will start to dive down when it loses its integrity.

Integrity is the most valuable asset to any company and the most appealing product to its customer.

Likewise, your integrity is the key aspect that will appreciate your value and put you at a point of advantage over others as you compete and interact in the marketplace. I will provide another example to illustrate how a lack of integrity works against you even without being aware of it.

I was recently shopping for an air ticket to go and visit our parents. The first travel agents I contacted gave me a very fair price quotation. However, being my first time using this travel agency, I decided to check it before transferring the funds to their account. During the process, I realized a few gaps in the information they had previously given to me. That raised questions of integrity, and since I could not be sure if this agency was genuine or not, I decided to end my dealings with them. I then contacted the company my family usually use to procure air tickets. Even though their prices were comparably high, I felt safer because I trusted their integrity; they always deliver, and they are dependable. When you engage in the success race, you must perceive integrity as an indispensable partner. When you have integrity, people will be happy to come to you irrespective of the competition in the industry. They will be more comfortable purchasing a reliable service at a higher fee than paying less for a service where they have doubt and feel insecure.

An empire built on dishonesty will sooner or later crumble. The temptation to get rich quick has lured so many would-be successful people into failures. The people who practice dishonesty are usually clever but not intelligent. They, therefore, use cunning means to pursue success aggressively and recklessly. The moral duty of uprightness is highly disregarded by such individuals. These fellows operate on the self-destruction principle of 'the end justifies the means'. In other words, they do not care how they obtain what they desire. Anything that seems to be an obstacle that stands in their way, they are ready to use any means to eliminate. Dishonesty becomes their most used tool to get their way through situations. Grabbing from others, fraud, failure to keep promises, defaulting on obligations, and misleading others are all aspects that eat out your would-be achievements.

Most people who end up being dishonest start as people of integrity. However, as they progress on the road to success, their uncontrolled desire to achieve turns into a monster that finally devours them. When you cease to look at success as a progressive process and want it instant and massive, you end up ruining your life. When you drop the moral campus and engage 'the end justifies the means' philosophy to achieve, you end in a huge crush. It is a self-destroying mistake to think that you can use and exploit people without facing the consequences. There is always a huge price that must be paid for using and exploiting people. This is the reason why people like Allen Stanford have fallen from glory to ashes. Apart from losing the now-defunct Stanford Financial Group empire, this once upon a time billionaire now languishes behind prison bars serving a one hundred and ten years prison sentence. While once upon a time Allen Stanford was among the richest men in America and indeed the world, he is now a penniless inmate. It does not matter how far fraud elevates you; the truth will one day place you where you rightly belong.

(vi) Aspiration sets the bar

Most people realize less, not because they are incapable of performing better, but because their conviction sets a ceiling on how high they can touch. Your aspirations and not the availability of opportunities will eventually decide the level of achievement. High aspirations will unlock doors of opportunities and allow you to navigate your way to new success. What a child envisions himself to be has a significant influence on who he eventually become as an adult. What will make you succeed is not having super brains but persistently putting to good use any calibre of brains that you have. An average mind that is persistently stretched is better than a genius mind that is underused.

(vii) Concentration

Your ability to focus on a few right things is key in enabling you to register success. Initiating and abandoning unfinished projects will grossly undermine your level of success. The point is, do not start a project unless you are willing to give it the attention and focus that it deserves. While by virtue of their personalities, some people may have a higher capacity to focus on a task and complete it, anyone can strengthen the habit of concentration if they apply it in everything they do. You cannot change your life or impact the world by amassing unfinished projects.

If you desire to succeed, you must acquire staying power. You need the stamina to hang in there and see the successful completion of what you started. Your ability to concentrate should not be determined by the ease or pleasure of doing the task. Instead, aspiration for excellence should give you the drive you need to push projects to completion regardless of the challenges involved. It is your level of concentration that will influence the ranking of the service you provide.

Know your point of strength

While an individual can possess many skills and be gifted with numerous talents, each person has only one point of strength. To sustainably succeed, you need to be aware of your point of strength because it provides a pivot upon which you hinge all your other abilities. If I were to use the human body analogy, your point of strength is as important as your brain.

Just as the entire body depends on the brain to function, so do all your other abilities depend on your point of strength to work synergetically to achieve success.

Your point of strength helps to illuminate your other abilities and become your identity icon in the marketplace. While nobody can be good at everything, everybody can excel at something. Therefore, your point of excellence becomes your point of strength. I will use the life of one of the world's most excellent swimmers to illustrate this point.

CASE ILLUSTRATION FIVE: MARILYN BELL

While many sportspeople will display some level of natural talent, this was not the case with Marilyn Bell. In fact, she at an early stage recognized that she was not a fast swimmer. However, the inability to swim fast did not discourage her from swimming. Soon she realized a unique ability that would overhaul her entire life. She discovered that though she was not a fast swimmer, she could stay in the water longer without getting tired. This was her point of strength and competitive niche against other swimmers. Coupled with her iron will, Marilyn capitalized on her ability to swim longer, which got her enrolled on the marathon swimming team. She never yielded to any challenge. If she faced an obstacle along her way to becoming a famous swimmer, she confronted the obstacle head-on, crushed it and pushed forward. She became unstoppable, and nothing was too huge to discourage her.

When Florence Chadwick, the nation's swimming champion, was offered $10,000 by Canadian National Exhibition (CNE) to swim across Lake Ontario, Marilyn took on the challenge to compete against her. Unlike Florence, her motivation was not the pay cheque but to fulfil her goal of doing something that nobody has ever done before. The promise to receive a $10,000 cheque at the end of the race could not sustain Florence's motivation, she dropped off when the going went tough. On the other hand, Marilyn's goal kept her motivated and moving. She was convinced that she could endure longer in water than any other swimmer, and she wanted to prove it to the rest of the world. Her desire to do something that no one else had ever done before kept her going. Her body was not strong enough, and neither was it well matured to carry her for twenty hours and fifty-nine minutes in cold, deep, and dangerous waters. But her iron will supported her more than the strongest muscles any swimmer could ever have. While her legs and arms felt floppy, her will was as strong as before starting the race. She had joined to win, and she resisted the option of giving up. Supported by her uncompromising coach, she swam her way to success.

At the age of sixteen, she set an unbreakable record as the first person to swim across Lake Ontario. The girl who started as a mediocre swimmer today has her name standing tall among the world best swimmers. In 1958, she found her place in Canada's Sports Hall of Fame and in 1993, she claimed her rightful spot in the Canadian Swimming Hall of Fame. Marilyn reached this far because she recognized her point of strength and put it to maximum use. Her other strength gravitated around it to create a synergy of strength that made her an unstoppable sports champion.

The point of strength success concept extends to the business world. Many successful businesses are built on this model. They grow their success on their point of strength, which is their competitive advantage over other companies in the same industry. For example, while many companies produce cars, each achieves success by providing a unique and exclusive element. Therefore, people who are looking for that particular aspect will be attracted to buying their product. For instance, while one company will focus on building an economical car, another company will provide a luxurious vehicle. Yet another will aim at creating a sporty car. Each of these companies will be seeking to attract a particular section of people to their products. That is why it may be hard to find a car with all the combinations of being economical, sporty, and luxurious. Companies know that by focusing on that one aspect, they will take their share of the market and drive themselves to success. This is why enterprises like Suzuki, Honda, Ford, Toyota, and the VW Group all operate in the same market, and each can attract customers. Each of these companies knows their point of strength that make them unique from the other producers. That is what keeps them in business.

Likewise, you need to know your point of strength that makes you unique from what other people are providing. It is that point of positive uniqueness that will enable you to carve out your space of success in an overcrowded market for those who have nothing inimitable to provide.

Appreciate the chain of success

While only you can start yourself on the road to success, you will need add-ons to make it to the plateau of success and remain there. Success works like a chain. You start with your dream. You dream alone, vision alone, set goals alone and envision the success you want to achieve alone. In this way, you are the pivot of the success that you desire to achieve. Doing all these things makes you the entrepreneur. However, you will need more heads to share your vision and goals when it comes to implementing your success. You will need more hands than you have. You will need to be present in more places than you can be. You will need more than one mind to plan, strategize and solve challenges. In other words, you will need a chain that you can attach yourself on to reach where you want to be. You will require people, and you will need a team to work with.

When you understand the chain of success, you will consider yourself the beginning joint of the chain. But to reach success, you will need many other joints added to you. You need more than one lens to see the future, therefore appreciate a team of visionary people to strategize with. You will require people to do marketing. You will need people in charge of controlling the quality of what you are offering, and you may even need someone to be in charge of your human resources. All together, these people make your chain of success. The quality of every joint in the chain matters. If there is a breakage in one joint, that one joint affects the entire chain's performance. It does not matter whether the chain's disjoined joint is in the middle or towards the end. A weakness in any part of the chain will decline its ability to function.

Likewise, it is with the people you add to yourself when you are pursuing success. Every employee is a part of the chain of success irrespective of where they are placed. The quality, commitment, dedication, loyalty and satisfaction of the people on your team will determine how effective your chain will be. I will give an illustration.

As part of our family tradition, we usually have a family

movie night after Sabbath. (If this is your first time to hear about Sabbath, it is a weekly day of rest and worship initiated by God in Genesis chapter two verses one to three. The theme of Sabbath rest runs through the Bible. It starts from Friday sunset to Saturday sunset. It is a weekly holiday which you can benefit from a lot. It will enable you to have that much-needed rest, connect with God and have quality time with loved ones. You can read more about the Sabbath in the Bible). Back to the movie night, our children like this moment because they eat popcorn and other treats. One Friday morning, I went shopping in one of the stores in preparation for the family movie night. Top on the list was a bucket of delicious and mouth-watering popcorn. As I headed straight to the section where popcorn is usually stocked, I was disappointed when I could not see any popcorn buckets on the shelves.

Our kids believe that a movie cannot be interesting unless they have bowls of popcorn on their laps. Therefore, going back home without the delicacy would have meant a miserable movie night for the children. Before moving to another shop, I decided to look for anyone working in the store and ask if they had popcorn in their storage. Soon I spotted a gentleman doing restocking in the freezer section.

After greeting him, I enquired whether they had some popcorn because stores are fond of this annoying habit of moving stuff around to different sections. He politely told me to go to the area I had already been to. It could be he thought that I was a new customer and did not know where to look. After telling him that I have already been where he was referring me to, and there is no single bucket of popcorn on the shelves, he put on a prominent apologetic face and said: 'I have plenty upstairs. How many buckets do you want?' He immediately dashed off. I was amazed by his attitude. What a fantastic employee! Does his boss, the owner of the store, know him? Does the millionaire at the top of the chain appreciate this man? Does he know that it is because of this man's likes, the people he may never meet, that he is achieving success? Does he appreciate that the millions in his business are made by men and women at the lower rank who keep his customers happy?

As I was still trying to understand, the super employee appeared with a box of popcorn. He looked very delighted for that sale as if the money was going straight to his pocket. I observed two things about this employee. First, he willingly went out of his way to serve a client from another section. Now, you may be wondering what is so special about that. In some stores, an employee will refuse to move from his designated area to assist you in looking for something in another section. Such employees have an indifferent attitude, and they do not hesitate to show it. They look and talk to you as if you had a fight with them the previous day. Their only relationship with the company is the pay cheque they receive at the end of the month. Beyond that, they do not care whether the company thrives or sinks. If it goes down, they move and look for another job. Unfortunately, most employees with such an attitude usually do not go far and never achieve great personal success.

Apart from going out of his way, the staff at this store made a striking response. He behaved as if he owned the store: 'I have plenty upstairs.' In his mind, he was part of the business. He was a piece, a joint, a part of the chain pulling this store to success. This is why he felt happy to see that this money did not leave the store to be spent elsewhere.

When you recognize and appreciate how the chain of success works, you will appreciate and treat everybody who works for you with respect. You will not perceive some as low-rank employees and others as high-rank executives. Instead, you will perceive them all as joints in your chain and their placement determined by the unique strength each one brings.

When it comes to hiring, you will handle the process carefully. You will not take on anybody because they are less expensive to hire. Your criteria for employing people will be based on the strength the person brings to your chain. You will pay attention to the quality of the joint you are adding to your chain. This will be at all levels beginning from the lowest job to the highest office in your enterprise. You will know that people who contribute to your success have value they bring to you, and you will be glad to appreciate that value in the way you treat and pay them.

When you appreciate the value of the chain of success, you can achieve at any level

The principle of appreciating people on your chain of success will enable you to develop a character that values other people, great or small. You will acknowledge the contribution they make towards your intended success. The case of Noah, a schoolboy from Cornwall, provides a good illustration of this principle.

One day, in 2017, while sitting on a sofa at his home, Noah found a plastic comic nose used the previous year. This bothered the youngster who believed that though used for a noble cause, the generous production of such materials and the irresponsible way they were disposed of was hurting the environment. Noah wanted to put that to an end, but he knew that he could not do that alone. He needed some add-ons to himself to cause the change that he desired. He needed to form a chain that would lead to the successful outcome he envisioned. His beginning point was the school council, where he was a member. He shared his concern with the school council members about the need to stop using plastic comic noses and replace them with noses made of non-plastic materials. Initially, the progress was slow, and nothing much was being achieved. However, he and the other children on the school council kept the vision of having non-plastic comic noses alive.

Before leaving the school to join secondary, Noah handed over the button to six-year-old Lauren to keep the fire for change alive. Lauren nagged the school administration so much, and they had to act. As a result, letters were written to members of the parliament, Sir David Attenborough and Mr Richard Curtis, the comic nose relief founder. Time passed, but the children never gave up their dream of using non-plastic comic relief noses one day. Some of the kids took it a step further by coming up with possible models of red noses made from non-plastic materials.

The efforts of the children paid off. One day the school received a letter from Comic Relief stating that plastic comic relief noses were replaced with non-plastic comic relief noses. In March 2021, all comic relief noses used in the United Kingdom were a hundred percent plastic-free! Thus, the chain of success started by one young boy in 2017 materialized into great success in 2021.

Way back in 2017, Noah identified a problem. He realized that he needed a chain to pull his envisioned success.

He created one by joining himself to his school council. By involving members of the parliament, Sir David Attenborough and Mr Richard Curtis, super hinges were added to the chain the children needed to achieve their success. Noah's case clearly demonstrates that the chain of success can make you perform at the top level. The chain of success made it possible for the idea started by a boy seated on a sofa in his home to change how things were to be done in an entire country.

Understanding the value of a zero

It was our daughter's birthday; she was turning ten. Our kids, like all other children, are usually excited about their birthdays. In fact, they start to remind us six months in advance that it will 'soon' be their birthday. However, this time, the focus of the reminder was not on the type of presents desired, as is usually the case. Instead, the emphasis was on the figure, the digits in the years that were being achieved. I remember two days toward her birthday, our daughter came looking for me. When she found me, she said, 'Mama, finally! I am moving from the single-digit babyish figure to more mature two-digit figures!'

She played and stood between the two helium-filled giant balloons on her birthday, representing digits one and zero to make the number ten, which was the age she had achieved. Without her noticing it, the zero balloon floated away, and she remained standing beside the one-digit balloon. I heard her shouting: 'Mama, my zero balloon has drifted away. This is awful, Mama; I now look like I am only one year old! Please, help me get my zero back'! The zero balloon had attached to the ceiling above her head, and she desperately needed it back to regain her age value. After giving the zero balloon back to my daughter, she hugged it and said, 'Phew! I am ten again'!

That was intriguing; it triggered me to think about the actual value of zeros in one's life. I wondered how many things people do not attach importance to but are the very things that matter the most. The zeros in our lives are the things that give us value and enable us to make value out of other things.

Digit 1 on its own is of very little value. Most people will not be very much bothered if they misplaced a £1 coin. In fact, if you go to a store with £1, you may not get much. Even when offered to a child, they will know that £1 is not a big deal of value. However, the power of zero can mysteriously transform £1 into fantastic value. When you have a £1 and put a 0 in the correct place value, you get £10. When you add another 0, you get £100. And if another 0 is added, the value rises to £1,000. Yet the addition of an extra 0 further appreciates the value to £10,000. If you put another 0, you get £100,000. Another 0 added will turn the figure to £1,000,000. If you put another 0 to the figure, it converts to £10,000,000. When another 0 is added, the value changes to £100,000,000. And one more 0 added will skyrocket the value to 1,000,000,000. The mystery of the place value of zero is astounding. The side on which you place the 0 determines whether it adds substantial value or becomes nothing.

Recognize the zeros in your life

The zero-value principle applies to building your success. You may not consider things valuable because of your perception or the place you have assigned them in your mind. The things that you ignore could be the things that helped other prominently successful people to become who they are. The difference between achievers and people that do not achieve is where they place the zeros in life. The placement of your zeros will determine the value you get from them.

As mentioned before, the zeros in your life are those things that give you value and enable you to make value out of other things. Most often, such things are taken for granted, ignored or misunderstood to be of no value. I will point out a few examples of the things you may consider to be 0s but have a tremendous capacity to impact your success.

(a) Your life

I know that this may sound ridiculous, but have you ever bothered to find out the monetary value of your body? Well, whether you are among the top rich or the poorest of the poor without a penny on your name, you are worth $45 million. I know that sounds unbelievable and even probably silly. However, according to *Wired* magazine, your bone marrow, lungs, DNA, kidneys, and heart as components are worth $45 million. The magazine states that if your entire body was to be valued, it is worth about $160 million. The purpose of referring to this data is to enable you to appreciate the value of your body. However, in real life, you are much more worth than that. Your mind alone can generate ideas that, when properly implemented, can result in billions of pounds. Though at times perceived as a zero, your life is an inexhaustible bank of resources. The entire wealth is in your mind.

In chapter four, we shall look at the personal tree of success. Under this model of attaining success, life is seen as the taproot to your achieving. Unfortunately, many people have become failures because they could not appreciate their lives as a resource. While such individuals continue to cry for lack of resources, they miss the point that it is life that converts other things into wealth. Under the personal tree of success model, life is the taproot, and it is perceived as the license that you need to operate on the street of success.

Dead people do not make wealth. Therefore, perceiving your life as the most critical resource you need to succeed is one of the fundamental character traits you need to succeed. When you appreciate your life as a vital resource, you can face any storm and any loss and still be successful. When you understand life as a resource, you will use it to build your success from nothing to greatness. In short, once you have life, you can embark on attaining any dream. The world presents numerous examples of great people who had no other resource but their lives and used them to build incredible success.

The first example of such people is Dr Wayne Dyer. A life filled with a positive attitude was the sole asset that Dr Dyer used to propel himself to success. In fact, as a child, his prospects to succeed should have been none. His father abandoned his mother when he was only three years old. His early childhood years were dominated by hardships as he stayed in the orphanage and foster homes. However, young Wayne knew that he had one asset with him, his life, and he decided to put it to good use. During his lifetime, he stood tall among influential persons of the 21st century. Irrespective of the fact that he inherited nothing from the father he never knew, his estate carries a net worth of $20 million. The difference between poverty, influence and success was the place he assigned the zero in his life. He attached value to it, and his life was overhauled.

Another example is Brian Tracy. He had an impoverished childhood. His family depended on charity for clothing. His early working years were challenging and exhausting. For instance, he worked as a construction labourer and lived in a small, freezing room. However, life changed when he decided to give himself the right value by investing his life where it would generate the best returns. Brian used the only resource he had, his life, to transform himself from who he was to whom he wanted to be. The moment he realized that only he was responsible for the life he wanted to live, he converted his life into an invaluable asset. Today, Brian stands as one of the most powerful motivational speakers. While he started with nothing in terms of material things, he has managed to appreciate his net value to $15 million by placing the zero in the right place.

The Issa brothers, Mohsin and Zuber, are fascinating proof of the tremendous value of life and how this asset that many perceive to be a zero can transform one's destiny. The two brothers did not grow up in plenty. Their parents immigrated from India in the 1960s. Like any other immigrant family, they grew up amidst the common challenges that any immigrant family would generally face. However, the difference between these two and other descendants of immigrant is the way they perceived life. The two brothers were focused, perceived life as an asset and set clear goals that would take them where they wanted to reach. They did not have plenty, but they had respect for honest labour. They used their lives as assets to work hard, save and attain the success that only a few can dream of. The Issa brothers prove that when you put zero in the correct place value, any dream is achievable.

When talking about how they achieved their success, Zuber,

the youngest of the two brothers, says: *'We grew EG from nothing. We've been on pumps, we've been stocking shelves, cleaning the toilets. You do everything.'* Twenty years after they bought their first petrol station at a value of £150,000, the two brothers have a net worth of £3.56 billion. These are men who you would have two decades ago found stocking shelves or cleaning a toilet. They currently own over six thousand petrol stations worldwide. In October 2020, they bought the giant superstore ASDA from Walmart. The Issa brothers are ordinary men who realized the extraordinary value of life and invested their lives in the right places. These two were not born into wealth. They used the asset called life, which many people consider to be zero, to achieve tremendous success.

You may till now have taken life for granted and never attached any value to it as an asset. Life is one of those things you may not give special attention to and never appreciate. While you may be working very hard to build your success, it is possible that you hardly notice your life as the most critical asset. It may be that you perceive it as a zero and have placed it in the wrong place value where it is yielding nothing for you. As you struggle to achieve, you may be paying attention to the figures, looking for tenders, making strategies to expand, overworking to excel, and overtaking your competitors. You may be overspending and depleting your life on things that do not matter or investing it in prospects that yield little. Yet, your life is the primary resource that you require to attain success. You need to be aware of the fact that your life is an exhaustible resource. If you misinvest it, overspend it, and worse of all, do not take care of it, it is possible to have it depleted, and you cannot get more out of it because nothing is left.

When you have a mindset that perceives life as a valueless zero, you take it for granted. You will go to sleep, wake up, go around your business, and never think of what if life stops. What would happen if that pump in your chest stopped? What about if your lungs stopped expanding and contracting? What about if those eyelids stopped moving up and down. What about if that red liquid stopped gushing up and down your body? What if that tap that drains the unwanted liquid out of your body stopped functioning? If you compare the time, resources, and attention you attach to other assets, you may realize that you are not aware of your life's value. Yet, your life is the most important asset. Minus your life, all the other assets would be meaningless to you. If you want to attain success, you must stay alive because dead folks do not work.

(b) The lives and health of other people

To become sustainably successful, you must develop a character that appreciates other people's life and health. When you understand that your success is enhanced or hindered by what is happening to others, you drop the character of being indifferent and adopt a caring personality. You stop perceiving people as meaningless zeros and instead place them where they are valuable.

You need to learn to perceive others' health as a universal asset and a part of your indirect assets. That mindset will enable you not to focus only on your own good but to impose upon yourself the duty of minding about the good of others. The effect of other people's lives and health on an individual's success can best be illustrated by the devastating COVID-19 economic and health impact. Although the pandemic started as a health issue, it has developed into a global social, economic and health crisis.

The COVID-19 era provides sufficient evidence that public health is a public asset that affects individual, enterprises, and the public. Before the pandemic, nations, multinational corporations, business tycoons, and individuals did not appreciate the magnitude of health as a local and universal asset. When the first COVID-19 case was announced in Wuhan, China in December 2019, the world was indifferent. Nobody cared about that health issue. The world perceived it as a Chinese problem. The Chinese government probably considered it a local problem for Wuhan city. And Wuhan city officials could have considered it as a problem for the sick person and his family. COVID-19 sprouted, grew, thrived, and overtook the world on the soils of indifference.

What started as a minor health issue, downplayed by the entire world, became a global economic and health monster. Within less than four months, COVID-19 overtook the world and forcefully captured the attention of nations great and small. It changed from being a health issue limited to one city and became a global social, health and economic crisis. Had the world perceived the first COVID-19 patients in terms of potential global loss, the current enormous human life and financial loss would have been avoided. The indifference initially exhibited when COVID-19 claimed its first victim has resulted in the loss of more than 2.3 million lives, and more lives continue to be lost. The IMF projects that the pandemic will cost the global economy up to $28 trillion. Besides, according to the International Labour Organisation, 195 million jobs are likely to be lost worldwide because of the pandemic. It is also expected that 2 billion people working in the informal sector are at risk of losing their jobs due to COVID-19. The said projections continue to be revised upwards as the pandemic claims more lives, destroys more livelihoods and wrecks more economies. What was initially considered to be nobody's business has wrecked world economies and turned the lives of billions of people upside down. Below is a story that illustrates the dangers of indifference.

The farmer, the rat, the rooster, the goat, the bull, and the snake

In this story, the farmer was getting upset by the rat, who found residence in his house. This rat was the naughty type who would disappear during the day and cause havoc during the night. The farmer would often be woken up by the noise of the rat as it nibbled on his harvest. As if that was not enough annoyance to the farmer, after filling its belly, the rat would turn the farmers living room into a gymnasium by running and jumping up and down the furniture. Every time the farmer tried to wake up and kill the rat, the rat would dash off, and the farmer would not know where it disappeared.

When the farmer had had enough mischief from the rat, he decided to look for its hiding place throughout the house. He moved every piece of furniture and checked every suspicious part. After a long search, he finally discovered a hole in the dark corner of the house. This was where his little tormentor would disappear for safety after wreaking havoc and disturbing his much-needed sleep. Satisfied that he had found the rat's hiding place, the farmer went to the nearby shop and bought a rat trap that he carefully placed at the hole entrance. Happy with his plan, the farmer left and went on with his business, knowing that this was the last night for the notorious rat.

The farmer placed the trap when the rat was out looking for food in the nearby bush. When it came back, it saw the trap just in time to avoid stepping on it. Since the rat could not remove the trap without being killed, it decided to look for help. So, it went to the rooster and explained its dilemma, hoping that the rooster would be of assistance. However, to the rat's disappointment, the rooster told the anxious rat that the trap was none of its business since it was happy with its life at the farmer's house. Disappointed, the rat decided to look for the goat, thinking that it would be kinder than the rooster had been. When the rat found the goat, with new optimism, it started to narrate its plight to the goat, who seemed not to pay much attention. Finally, when the goat raised its head from the yummy grass it was eating, it told the rat that it was happy with the way things were at the farm, and the trap was not its problem.

Once again, disappointed but unwilling to give up, the rat decided to look for help one more time. It headed for the barn where it knew it would find the bull. Knowing that the bull was its only remaining hope, the rat was careful how it narrated its plight. It did its best to make the bull understand the magnitude of its problem and pleaded with the bull for help. Finally, the bull, which all the time had its mouth submerged in the trough, stopped drinking. Looking down at the tiny rat, it said that it was sorry, but that was not his business. The bull told the disappointed rat that it liked it at the farm and was pleased with how the farmer took good care of him. Aggrieved, the rat decided to make a temporary bed in the barn corner where it miserably spent the night.

Unknown to the farmer was a snake who knew that there was a rat in the house, and it frequently tried to trap the rat, but every time it tried, the rat outsmarted the snake and escaped. The snake decided to come to the rat hole on this particular night and try its hunt again. Hearing the trap go off, the farmer jumped from his bed, knowing that he had finally got rid of that annoying rat. Since he very well knew where the rat trap was, he rushed in the dark without bothering to light the lamp. Reaching out for the trap, he felt that the weight was much more than that of a rat, and the creature in his hands was for sure not a rat. In a second, the creature was coiling on his hand. Before he could shake it off, he felt sharp fangs dig deep in the palm of his hand. A few hours later, the farmer died of snake poisoning. What had the previous day been a busy, happy farmhouse was now a place of mourning as neighbours, family members and friends gathered at the farm to mourn the farmer's death.

The rooster, the goat and the cow gathered in the barn where the rat was still hiding to mourn their master too. As the rat heard the animals talk about the cause of their master's death, it whispered: 'This would not be the case if you had helped me.'

As the elders planned the funeral, the rooster instinctively decided to go; 'Cock-a-doodle-doo.' The deceased's uncle said, 'How dare that rooster crow when its master is dead. Get it and slaughter it at once', he ordered one of the farmworkers. As the worker picked the rooster and took it for slaughter, the rat again whispered, 'This would not have been the case had you helped me remove that trap'.

As the elders progressed with the funeral preparations, the next item on the agenda was how to feed the mourners. In Africa, in-laws are usually treated to a nice meal both in good and sad times. Therefore, the elders decided that the goat should be on the menu for the deceased's in-laws. Soon the door of the barn swung open, and another worker took the goat for slaughter. The rat again whispered from its safe hiding, 'Only if you had accepted to help me, this would not be happening'.

Seeing that all his friends were taken to meet their premature death, the bull started to blame the rat; 'This is all your fault, you little naughty rat, you caused all this trouble. All my friends have to die because of you.' The little rat answered back, 'No, you are very mistaken; it is not my fault. I was trying to save myself, but you all ignored me. You thought the trap was my problem. Had you helped me remove the trap, the snake would have tried to hunt me the same way it usually does, and I would have outmanoeuvred it as I have always done. It would have gone back as a loser, and the farmer would still be alive. If the farmer was not dead, both the cock and the goat would not have to be slaughtered. They would be here, enjoying their lives at the farm as usual.' The rat paused for a second and continued. 'Well, maybe they would still have to die during one of those festivals, but certainly not at this time.' The bull listened and, in a sad voice, muttered, 'I guess you are right; I am just terrified right now. I wish I was as small as you are so I can hide from all this.'

Meanwhile, the elders continued with the planning of the farmer's funeral. When it came to feeding all the mourners, it was decided that the bull will make enough beef stew for everyone. Soon, the barn door swung for the last time. As the bull was being pulled away, it whispered, 'Goodbye, wise little friend. You were, after all, right. You will always be right; any problem on the farm is everybody's problem.'

Though the above story is just a tale, it carries with it critical moral lessons. You cannot seek to be successful while ignoring those around you. No one in life is too insignificant to matter. In early 2020, after COVID-19 started claiming lives in China, the World Health Organization's professional advice to the globe was that COVID-19 did not pose an international threat. The global health watchdog went on to say that the virus would disappear the same way SARS had disappeared. It remains a mystery how a professional body would be so confident in providing misleading advice. Probably someone did not think that it was such an important matter at the time. Maybe the person who handled the case was not competent enough. Perhaps the region involved, and the people affected did not mandate giving serious attention to the man-killer virus. The answers may never be found. However, what is visibly irrefutable is the havoc caused by something initially dismissed as too minor to attract the globe's attention. The loss, the brokenness and the scars left by COVID-19 have irreversibly changed the face of the earth. What was initially perceived as the 'rat's problem' has affected everyone on the 'farm' called planet earth.

Even giants need small people around them

When you mind and care about other people, you do a favour to yourself. I recently read facts of the case in which an organization received a grant from the Bill and Melinda Gates Foundation. (Unfortunately, the Gates are splitting. That may pose questions regarding their future collective philanthropy work.) But till now, Bill and Melinda Gates own the world's top private foundation.

The Bill and Melinda Foundation is very fundamental in supporting life and livelihoods in poor economies. You may hold a different opinion about the objective of Bill and Melinda Gates and other philanthropists. But, irrespective of personal views, what cannot be denied is that many millions of people worldwide have been positively impacted by Bill and Melinda's generosity. By their charitable actions, millions of poor children have had an opportunity to live and have productive lives. Poor communities have been given better prospects. All these are blessings that the Gates have bestowed on the world population. The question is not what would happen if Bill and Melinda became indifferent about the problems of the world? Everyone knows that millions of poor people would suffer and perhaps even die as a result. Therefore, there is no question about the world needing Bill and Melinda.

However, the critical question is, do Bill and Melinda need the world? Do poor people matter or make a difference in the lives of the world's fourth-richest persons. The answer is in the affirmative. Bill and Melinda may never see an increase in their bank statement that accrues from investing in helping those in need. However, the couple gets rewarded by accessing priceless things that money cannot buy. Nothing can buy the satisfaction of knowing that you helped another human being in need.

From the economic angle, when Bill and Melinda invest in improving people, they enable them to thrive. When individuals thrive, economies thrive too. Thriving economies support business. Therefore, in a way, the humanitarian arm, the Gates Foundation, supports its parent organization, the business arm, Microsoft. As said before, public health is a public asset. Business prospects may never have been their motive for supporting humanitarian causes, but Bill and Melinda know that the Microsoft business thrives in economies where people have improved quality of life.

If you want to achieve satisfying success, do not be indifferent to people. Know that even when they may initially appear to be zeros in your success, they will contribute to your success when they are given the correct place value. Some of the people whose lives improve due to the numerous charitable projects supported by the Bill and Melinda foundation become a part of the Microsoft market. As we all know, the more market a business gets for its products, the more it will thrive. That is one of the fundamental laws of commerce. Therefore, when you extend goodwill to the people, be it rich or poor, you, in a way, increase your own success. This principle applies in both business and humanitarian engagements. If you desire to achieve sustainable success, you must learn to value people without first assessing their price tag.

(c) Your family

Family is a vital aspect of your life. You are born and find yourself in a family or linked to one. Even children who find themselves in an orphanage or foster homes have a link to a biological family. For cases where there is no family trace, the individuals may live with the reality of the missing link between their existence and how they entered the world. Therefore, in a way, the family is an indispensable part of life.

There is a tendency to categorise families into 'right' and 'wrong' types. People tend to attach success to the 'right' family and failure to the 'wrong' family. However, there is a lot of myths involved in that kind of thinking. Success can be achieved as a result of pleasant or unpleasant things that are related to your family. Belonging to the 'right' family does not guarantee success, and neither does coming from the 'wrong' family warrant failure. Success can be achieved in both cases, and failure cannot be ruled out in either of the two. Irrespective of how you perceive your family, there might be some contribution it made to your success.

The focus is not on the 'right' family that gives you a good childhood, good education, a good CV and bequeaths you with wealth and a good name. If you belong to such a family, you probably already recognize its contribution to your success. I am focusing on the type many people would categorise as the 'wrong' family'. This is the family that many would not want to be identified with and wish they did not carry that name because of the disgrace it brings to them.

While your life is shaped by the choices and decisions that you take, the family you are born into is one thing that is predetermined for you. You just find yourself there, and you are connected or stuck with it for the rest of your life. No baby gets to choose its parents. You had no voice in whom your mother, father, siblings, or grandparents would be or how they would treat you or behave. While these people make your core group, they are a predetermined package that may totally differ from who you are and your values. Your family may not be the type that you are proud of or happy to associate with. Nevertheless, it is the only family that you have. Your parents may not be what you would have desired. In fact, they may be horrible people, but they are still your parents. Your siblings may have hurt you, they may be a disgrace, an embarrassment, but they remain your siblings. However despicable the people you call family may be, you are irreversibly connected to them.

Now, you have two options; option one is to write them off from your life and live as if they never existed. It is possible that as you work on your success, you may want to sever the cord that ties you to the 'wrong' family. You may feel embarrassed to be associated with who they are and what they do or have done. You, therefore, may choose to ignore them and pretend that they do not exist. You may try to replace them with new stronger bonds through marriages, friendships, and business. However, you will soon realize that you are embarking on an impossible task when you take that option. Even when you want to erase your family from your life, society will always throw it in your face. Your family is one of the things that are impossible to erase. You may be both physically and emotionally distanced from your family. Still, society will keep an active connection between you and the family you belong to. The reality has always been that the more you run away from your family, the more society will be happy to connect you with it. This has been the case in the past, and most of us agree that it is still the same today. Whether classy or common, glamorous or disgraceful, family is too big to be pushed under the carpet.

However, you have the second option: to try and find the good in your family. However tiny, there will always be a small good something in your family. However useless, embarrassing, and repugnant your family may seem to be, there is a role it played in your success. Some of the contributions may have been too ordinary for you to notice, yet you would not be who you are without that. For instance, if you look at a mother, she may not have had any material wealth to give you. However, the fact that she breastfed/bottle-fed you, washed your clothes, cooked your meals, and cared for you when you could not do those things for yourself makes her a part of your success team. If you have a father who has many vices but managed to pay your tuition, you will appreciate him for that. You will not write him off because of his many mistakes. You will know that your success empire sits on the basic education that he paid for. If you have siblings that have messed up their lives and disgraced themselves, you will not write them off to keep an impressive and clean public image. When you look back, you may see that there are bridges in life you would not have crossed had it not been for the support you got from your now 'wasted and useless' siblings. It may be the protection they gave you or the care they provided. It may be any of those small things that we usually do not notice but matter a lot when your wellbeing depends on another person.

It will help if you try to look at your family with a new lens. It will make a lot of difference when you accept that it is alright to have a family different from what you wished. This is because things that influence your success can come in negative or positive packages or even both. When the right mindset is applied, negative experiences in life are as powerful as positive experiences in motivating you to succeed.

If you have a father who abandoned you or a mother who dumped you at the orphanage doorsteps, it is common sense to look at them as useless in your life. While it is justifiable to think of a mother who abandoned you as cold-hearted and irrelevant in your life, it is also possible to have a different perception of her. Despite her actions, you will change your opinion when you look for the good in her. It is possible to think that nothing good can come from such a mother, and it is okay for you to feel that way. However, when you purpose to seek the good in such a mother, it is there; she gave you a chance to live. As we said before and shall see in chapter four, Life is the primary and most essential resource you need to succeed. The mother who dumped you at the orphanage gave you one precious gift; she gave you life. She allowed you to be born.

I know that there is an argument that the quality of life matters in attaining success. That is true. But it is also true that people who are not given a chance to be born cannot succeed. It is also true that people have made it from the worst quality of life to success. The good that I want you to see in the mother that abandoned you is that she did not terminate you when you were still a fetus in her body. She kept the pregnancy. That may appear to be nothing, and you may even say that you never asked her to conceive you. While that is true, you will also be aware that some mothers do not allow their unborn children to see the sun. Many pregnancies that would have resulted in successful people get terminated every day. So, if your mother made a choice to give birth to you, appreciate her for that. She gave you a chance to fight for your success. Do not spend the rest of your life resenting her for abandoning you, placing you for adoption or having you end up in a foster home. That woman that you may know or never see gave you a chance to be born. Appreciate her for that because only living people can achieve success. If you have such a mother, recognize her. She could have considered the option of ending the life in her body, but she chose to preserve it.

The scenario of being abandoned by a mother is one of the extreme cases. If something positive can be found even in such a case, you can also find something positive about your family. A changed mindset will enable you to realize that no matter how much your family may have let you down, it contributed to your success. A mindset that appreciates both positives and negatives in life will enable you to perceive your family differently.

You will understand that the raw materials that build your success come from both good and bad experiences that you go through. You do not have to have a clean family to become successful. The negatives in your family may be the drivers of your success. For instance, if you had a lazy father who did not do much to provide for you, that may be the driving force to your hard work. If you came from a bitter family, that might have given you the resolve to have a happy family and give your spouse and children all the love you have. Suppose you suffered the impact of your parents divorcing, that may have sealed your determination to raise your children in a happy marriage.

I have a friend whose father changed wives as often as he changed his cars. When we talked about her soon coming marriage, my friend shared with me how hard it was to grow up in a family where she had to get used to women walking in and out of her father's life. She told me how adjusting to her father's numerous wives' various governments was nerve-wracking for both her and her siblings. And as if covenanting with herself, she muttered, 'I am getting married once, and forever'. After many years of marriage, my friend is as happy as a newlywed.

In my friend's case, instead of shaking her faith in marriage, the negative experience of her father's dysfunctional marriages helped her to work for a stable and happy marriage. Although my friend came from a repeatedly broken home, she positively used the lessons to achieve a happy family. She learned from her parents the high cost of broken relationships. It is those lessons that made her resolve to succeed in her own marriage.

If you desire to become a successful, happy person, avoid perceiving your family as a useless zero. Your family is part of what makes you. No matter how insignificant and it does not matter if their contribution was positively or negatively packaged, they have a role in making you. Therefore, do not lose them. Like a zero adds value to a one when placed in the correct place value, so it is with your family. The value you attain by recognizing and embracing your family does not have to be monetary or tangible. It may be the priceless peace of mind that comes with knowing that you are at peace with everyone, including your family members.

Chapter three

Pressure, an invaluable ally in achieving success

To achieve outstandingly, you need to appreciate the role of pressure in launching you from being ordinary to becoming extraordinary. When you work with pressure, it becomes a great asset and enables you to achieve the unachievable. On the other hand, when you fight pressure, it becomes a liability and an enemy that eventually pulls you down. Therefore, you need to learn to cooperate with pressure rather than fight it. In life, there are three pressure sources. These are:

1. Pressure from self

2. Pressure from other people

3. Pressure from your environment

The Pressure Pyramid Theory of Success (PPTS)

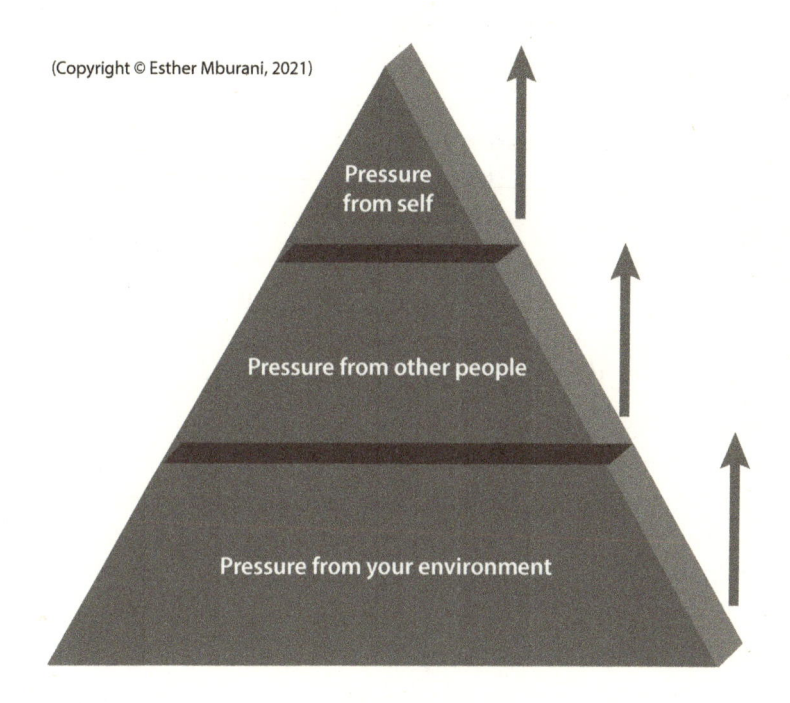

(Copyright © Esther Mburani, 2021)

- Pressure from self
- Pressure from other people
- Pressure from your environment

Pressure from your environment

Pressure from your environment represents negatively pre-determined things. For instance, you are born in a disaster-prone area. You are born in a developing country. You are born in a low caste. You belong to a disadvantaged race or tribe. You are born with a disability. You are orphaned at a tender age, and so on. You have no contribution in causing the pressure that you experience from these factors. What you face is pre-determined, and you find yourself in the middle of it.

The critical role of this type of pressure is that it causes meaningful awareness of your situation. It makes you feel uncomfortable with what is happening. It kindles in you the passion for creating the type of change that will move you from your undesirable situation to your dream position. When properly utilised, pressure from your environment provides a nursery bed for your dreams to germinate by triggering the visioning process.

However, beyond that, pressure from your environment cannot on its own change your situation. This explains why many people will complain about their bad situation but remain in it. While they are aware of their environment, they do not do what it takes to get out of it. This means that pressure from your environment can only be useful if it pushes you into action. People who have no feasible action plans on dealing with pressure from their environment end up sharing their dreams but never living them.

Pressure from other people

The second level on the pyramid is pressure from other people. These will include family members, employers, employees, workmates, peers and friends, among others. This type of pressure is helpful because it creates awareness in terms of expectations, ideals, and standards and brings you face-to-face with competition. Pressure from other people ignites in you a desire to excel and sharpens your focus.

Dependent on your response, pressure can thrust you to success or pull you down to a bottomless pit of inadequacy. While pressure from other people can trigger your desire to succeed, such success is likely to be short-lived. You can gain sustainably from the pressure from other people only when you convert it into personal motivation. While people may ask you to work harder and push you by challenging your capabilities, none of that can sustainably change you into a successful person. Pressure from other people is only helpful if it can inspire, motivate, compel or even agitate you into positive, decisive planned actions.

Pressure from self

When you look at the pressure pyramid, pressure from self occupies the smallest space compared to the space occupied by pressure from your environment and the pressure from other people. You will also note that there is no thick barrier between this pressure and success on the pyramid. This means that only the pressure you exert on yourself will free you from all the factors holding you back. Thus, it is pressure from self that will give you the thrust you need to turn your dreams into your desired reality. Your inner motivation will provide you with an intense passion and an unstoppable drive to achieve. Perhaps this explains why successful people never lose momentum to pursue success.

Here is a simple example of how pressure from self works. Our ten-year-old daughter is a brilliant girl. She, however, at times is reluctant in taking the initiative to do things. At times, she gets distracted and diverts to something else and takes more time to complete an assigned task. Our children are expected to tidy up. This has turned out to be a pressure point in their lives because we never stop reminding them to do that.

After the family evening prayer, we usually take our kids to bed and tuck them in. On one occasion, I noticed that our eldest daughter had not kept the bedroom tidy irrespective of the fact that she had been reminded. However, instead of feeling frustrated, I decided to talk with our daughter. I told her that everything she does or does not do contributes to the character she will eventually have. I explained to her the fact that if she desires to become a responsible adult, her beginning point is to be a responsible child. I let her know that she was encouraging a habit that she may struggle to break later in life by not tidying up her room. While I was talking, I noticed that she was paying more attention than she usually would. After that, we knelt beside her bed and prayed together. I kissed her goodnight and tucked her in.

When I woke up, the house was super tidy. The entire house was remarkably in order. The living room was spotless, the laundry was folded, the kitchen rack was empty, and the Bibles, devotion book and hymns put on the table, ready for the morning worship. She also had filled my water bottle that I usually take to the gym. She put a note on the table indicating that she had completed all the tasks at 4:12 am. Our daughter is usually a hefty sleeper who will not wake up from her sleep for any reason. It was astounding to see that she could wake herself up during such early morning hours and do all those chores without anyone asking. Only pressure from self could make our daughter accomplish that much at such an hour and by herself. While we appreciated and acknowledged the drastic transformation she was achieving, we did tell her that she did not have to go to that extreme. We encourage our children to have a balanced approach in all aspects of life to avoid burnouts.

The only force that can sustainably launch you to success

is the pressure that you exert on yourself. That becomes your inner drive to achieve. Once you possess that drive, it results in an unquenchable desire to succeed. Pressure from self makes you respond to the pressure from your environment and pressure from other people in a way that positively changes your life. However, you need to guard against the yoyo type of pressure. When you stop to positively relate with pressure from yourself, you may find that you are dropping down to failure faster than you rose to success.

Surprisingly, successful people never cease to relate to pressure positively. That is what drives them to keep appointments, maintain strict schedules and wake up early irrespective of the fact that they already achieved all they desire. To maintain what you have, you must keep the personal pressure gauge at the optimum.

The pressure synergy

The three types of pressure work together in transforming you into a successful person. Pressure from your environment and pressure from other people becomes a catalyst to success when it activates the pressure from yourself. When the plug on pressure from self is pulled, it thrusts you to unstoppable success.

It is essential to establish how you relate to the three types of forces to your advantage. Some people will advise you to avoid pressure stating that it is not good for your health. However, the fact is, pressure is not bad in itself; the problem is how people respond to it. When you learn the art of using pressure to your advantage and know how to relate to it healthily, it will never be a problem for you. Any life void of pressure becomes docile, routine common and stunted.

When properly used, pressure becomes the most effective catalyst in making you a successful person. For instance, a CEO who experiences pressure from his board members because of a substandard report will likely give a better report in the next board meeting. Likewise, an athlete who fails to win a medal will likely shine out in the upcoming tournament if he uses his fans' support as positive pressure. He will exert more pressure on himself during subsequent training to meet the expectations of his fans.

At times, negative pressure from people is all that you need to propel you to unmatched achievements. Gabby Douglas is an outstanding American artistic gymnast. She is an icon of success in the world of sports. She shone brightly in the 2012 Olympics when she emerged as the all-around champion. She has been a member of gold-winning teams in world championships. She was on the team of the 'Fierce Five' and the 'Final Five'. Gabby uses pressure from self to excel and pressure from other people to push herself. This is reflected in one of her quotes when she says:

'Gold medals are made out of sweat, blood, and tears and efforts in the gym every day.' [22]

This quote seems to imply that her success is more of a result of hard and focused work than mere talent. The desire to emerge as the best and stand out from the rest motivates her to push herself. The pressure to win activates her energy reserves and propels her to achieve above her competitors.

It is the pressure to become, the pressure to be, the pressure to achieve, the pressure to prove, the pressure to disprove, the pressure to solve, the pressure to change, the pressure to help, the pressure to intervene, the pressure to provide, the pressure to make a difference, the pressure to preserve, the pressure to protect and the list goes on, that will push you into action and achievement. Accomplishment becomes minimal in the absence of pressure. In a way, it all boils down to choice. You can choose to embrace pressure and leave your footprints on the path you walk in the journey called life, or you can avoid pressure and leave nothing behind. Once you learn the art of relating constructively to pressure, it becomes an excellent resource that pushes you to higher success.

Chapter four

Determine the person you want to be

Know your value

Every person has two values: the perceived value and the actual value. The perceived value is the value other people assign to you. Society assigns value by looking at what you have and who you are. That becomes your perceived value. This type of value can be deceptive when compared to who you indeed are.

However, your actual value is the value that you attach to yourself. There may be a significant variation between your perceived value and your actual value. What will make you succeed in life is the value you assign yourself. Your actual value will give you determination and stamina to confront challenging situations as you map your way to success. While the perceived value may be exciting and propel you for a while, it usually diminishes when faced with challenging situations. This is because people will assign you a value only when you are riding high and withdraw it as soon as you start to descend low.

While your perceived value is linked to externals, your actual value emanates from your character. Your actual value defines who you are. However, you need to be aware of controllers, manipulators and users who will want to assign you a value that allows them to achieve their agenda. For example, users will massage your ego to get you into doing what they want. This was the case with King Darius in the Bible when the governors stroked his ego and led him to make a decree that he later regretted. To pull Daniel down, the governors suggested to the king that all people in the kingdom pray only to him for thirty days. In this way, the bitter governors were able to use the king's ego to eliminate Daniel.

Users will want to inflate your ego to have their way. Users will usually want to control you by replacing your actual value with a depreciated perceived value. However, you need to know that whether you will move up or you will move down will largely depend on how you perceive yourself in life. In short, you will become the person that you believe you are.

Self-packaging

Life is one huge marketplace where every individual must market themselves. No matter how much the market may be circulated, people will not ignore you when you are the best available. The way you package yourself determines the price you attract. Therefore, not only learn but also master the art of packaging yourself irresistibly. If you want to achieve and maintain a high value, you need to aim at doing the best. People may not like your skin colour, your race, the way you look or speak. But you give them no choice if you are the best available. They must take you, not on their terms, but your terms. When you are the best, you free yourself from the shackles of racism, classism and any other obstacle that would have held you back.

People who carved their space globally and became known

for what they achieved were not satisfied with the expected standard of success. Your aim should not be the highest that has ever been achieved but at the highest that has never been achieved. Your motivation should be to break the record and write your own. It is within your mandate to package yourself in the way you desire the world to know you. You can discard the price tag imposed on you by other people and determine the one that matches your true worth. I will use the experience of a young student to illustrate this point.

CASE ILLUSTRATION SIX: HELENA

Helena had just got her exams results, and she was not happy with the scores. She knew that she could achieve better grades than what was on her exam results slip. So, she walked to a nearby high school and asked the headteacher if he could allow her to register at his school and retake the exams. After calmly explaining her request to the headteacher, she received the following response.

'I don't entertain failures in my school. Now, get out of my office! I need to attend to other people who are waiting.'

With a saddened heart, Helena started on her way out. As she held the door handle, before she could step out of the office, she turned and walked back towards the headteacher, who looked puzzled by her rather unexpected behaviour. With eyes fixed on him, Helena spoke in a gentle but assertive voice.

'Sir, I am not a failure. I want better grades than I have.'

She walked out feeling great because she had not accepted to carry the 'failure' tag that the headteacher was attempting to assign her. Helena's courage, focus and resolve to pursue her success resonates with what happened during the Euro 2020 final match. On Sunday, the 11th of July 2021, during the Euro 2020 final presentation ceremony, some young England players removed the silver medals before they landed on their necks. This act was interpreted in many ways by fans and the wider public. However, it may have been a bold self-addressing message to say that, 'I will not settle for silver.' To become a game-changer in your life, you must have the intelligence, boldness and assertiveness to confront situations that want to pull you down. You must know the cost and be willing to pay the price of what it takes to put your life back on track. You must have the courage to reject a tag below your dream.

Self-packaging means that you need to learn to achieve in a manner that will not necessitate you to explain your achievements by attaining achievements that speak for themselves. Self-packaging or self-repackaging is not something that happens overnight. It is a journey and a process that begins with one step followed by a million others in the right direction.

To move from an undesired situation, you must have the courage to sever all the cords that connect to excuses. You cannot progress until you get enough courage to face the fact that only you, hold yourself back from achieving. Clinging to excuses is one of the significant hindrances to attaining success.

Be intentional in connecting with God

'I can do all things through Christ who strengthens me.' [23]

When the above becomes your motto, you will be able to face and soar above any life crisis. The phrasing in this verse implies that all things can be done when Christ is the source of your strength. The word 'all' gives no exemption. When you are anchored to Christ, His presence changes you. His power living in you provides you with strength, motivation, determination, hope and courage to face all situations with an overcomer's mindset. When you are on God's team, you can pull through any situation.

People who approach the throne of God with doubt usually give up when He was just about to make things happen for them. One thing that God never promises us is instant solutions to our situations all the time. Neither does He promise to provide the type of solutions that we already have in our minds. At times, God's answers are instant, and at other times they are not. God has a mind; He does not have to answer us according to what we think. He always provides the best to each person according to the plan He has for that individual. When we trust and wait, we shall come to realize that God's way was, after all, the best. I will use an illustration to further explain this point.

CASE ILLUSTRATION SEVEN: GABBY

Gabby was dating Jim for some time. She truly believed that Jim was the man she desired to have for a husband. Therefore, she always prayed and asked God that her relationship with Jim would mature into a marriage. However, at some point, Jim decided to break up with Gabby and married Jenny.

Gabby was disappointed because she thought that Jim loved her as much as she loved him. Irrespective of her disappointment, Gabby's faith in God did not waver. She continued to trust God and believed that He had a plan for her life. After some time, unfortunately, Jim passed away, leaving Jenny as a young widow. Meanwhile, God had blessed Gabby with a loving fiancé who later married her. Every time Gabby looked back at how God guided her life, she acknowledged that His ways are better than her ways.

Trust in God does not insulate you from the hard times of life. It only guarantees you to be an overcomer of the challenges you face. In Christ, there are no losers. Any loss for those who are in Christ is a post-dated gain. There are times when God will seem not to care, but those are the moments when He cares for you the most. God may allow the bread to be taken away from your plate because He intends to serve you a cake. However, you need to remain patient during those moments when you will have to wait for what God is going to provide. Your faith will be most tested when your plate is empty, and you wait upon God to provide. The waiting time may be the most complicated time to go through. However, in the end, God will make things work out for your good.

Going through hard times does not mean that there is something wrong with you. I recently attended a women's workshop where one of the participants shared her challenging experience of waiting for a husband. She wanted to encourage other single ladies who were still waiting. This lady is, by all standards, beautiful and attractive. In her testimony, she pointed out that she had to wait for forty-seven years and two days before she could marry the man God created for her. From the way she talked, it was evident that she is happily married and deeply in love with her man. Her waiting was not in vain.

In His infinite wisdom, there are things that God will not rush just because you are asking. If God keeps you waiting for something or He does not provide it, there is a good reason for that. You may for a while or till eternity not be able to know the reason. However, when everything is finally revealed, you will appreciate that God did the right thing for you. When you ask God to intervene in your situation, you need to know that while He cares for your feelings, He also pays attention to the bigger picture. He looks at your life in totality and what He does is for your ultimate good.

God's wisdom is above your understanding. Can you imagine the type of parent who would give the child everything the child asks? At times, a child will ask and even cry for dangerous things that can hurt her. A caring parent will say no to his child when the toddler is screaming for a knife and instead give her a soft cuddly toy. In the same manner, God will see beyond your desires that have the potential to harm you and instead provide what is right for you. If all the time God acted according to our wishes, our lives would be a total mess. Therefore, you need to understand and appreciate that His thoughts are far superior to your thoughts.

Allow God to take control

When you come to God for help, you should be willing to step away from the driver's seat and take the passenger seat. You need to trust Him and allow Him to navigate the way even though your life may seem to be heading straight into the 'red sea'. You need to believe that He can create a road for you in the middle of the sea. He said that:

'When you pass through the waters, I will be with you, and when you pass through the rivers, they will not sweep over you.' [24]

God did not promise to protect you from passing through the raging sea. He knows that, at times, the path you must take to success will make you go through the rough waters of life. However, when your life is in His hands, you will be safe despite the intense waves that may be raging all around you.

Present your plans to God as proposals

While it is okay to come to God with a plan, you should present it as a proposal. You need to allow Him to have an independent opinion on what you are presenting. You should have the understanding that after God looks at your submission, He will do that which is most suitable for you. Therefore, your proposal can be given a yes, can be modified, delayed, or rejected. When you trust God enough to know that what He does is in your interest, you will be willing to follow His will. You should never come to God with a plan that is already sealed. He will not allow you to use Him to stamp strategies that will end up hurting you. The reason you may feel disappointed with God's decision could be because you leave Him out during the planning phase. You only want Him to come in at the execution stage. It is presumptuous to have a plan that is potentially harmful to you and is against God's will, and you ask Him to be part of it. I will give an illustration.

At my former place of work, part of my duties was to countersign the cheques. The cheques had to be accompanied by satisfactory paperwork, which I needed to read before I could endorse. However, there were times when the Cashier would bring a big pile of cheques and tell me that she was in a hurry to go to the bank before closing time. (That was way back before electronic banking was widely in use.) That meant that

I should sign the cheques without reading the attached paperwork. When such a request would be presented, no matter how urgent she said the cheques were, I never rushed into signing. I would tell her that I cannot endorse what I have not read and agreed to because affixing my signature made me responsible and accountable. However, that also meant that, at times, I would be misunderstood for being too bureaucratic. But this, at times, saved the organisation from making expensive mistakes.

Without being presumptuous, I have used the above example as an illustration to show that because God cares for you, He will not endorse plans that push you into trouble. If God expects you to hold specific values, you cannot present to him a proposal that tramples on the values you are to uphold and you expect a yes from Him. Although God does not abandon us when we make mistakes, we would avoid a lot of trouble if we right from the beginning involved Him in our plans. Each choice, each action, comes with consequences, good or bad. When you involve God from the start, He provides what is in line with the blueprint that He has for your life. This is the reason why He says:

'I know the plans that I have for you.' [25]

Allowing God to be part of your plans will save you from making regrettable mistakes.

Chapter five

The personal tree of success model

This model looks at personal success as a process that involves releasing what is within you. The model gets its inspiration from the procedure a seed has to undergo before it can bear fruit. A seed that remains intact and does not experience the cracking process will not release the embryo inside it. The embryo in the seed represents the potential that you were created with. That potential cannot be activated and therefore become useful to you unless you deliberately engage in the process that allows your abilities to crack out of their cage. Like a tender embryo needs nurturing, your abilities need to be cultivated and developed to become productive.

According to this model, success is homegrown in you. It is an in built hibernating potential that you are born with. When you understand this model, you will recognize that success is something you bring with you to this world and not something you acquire from the world. The world is just an environment where you are given the opportunity to share what only you can give.

The seed and the cracking process

One of the fundamentals of this approach to understanding success is the *seed* and *cracking* principle. While everyone is born with the *seed* of success, that *seed* cannot amount to anything unless the cracking process occurs. To be able to produce, the seed must go through the tough process of cracking. A seed that does not crack ends up rotting because its embryo remains trapped within. The cracking process launches the seed on the journey to transform into a plant that yields more of its kind.

Once planted, a seed must undergo the hibernating phase. The hibernating period may be seen as an inactive stage in the development of a seed. However, while this may seem to be a dormant stage, it is also when the seed experiences chemical changes that allow it to germinate into a plant. The cracking process takes place when the seed is under the dirt/soil. To become a plant, the tender embryo must push its way in two directions. The radicle must grow downward to give the plant water and nutrients, and the shoot system must grow upwards so that the plant can get sunlight. The cracking and germination phase is challenging in the life of a plant. This phase requires resilience from the plant to push through the barrier beneath and above to thrive.

You must know that success does not come without intentionality. The cracking process sets you on a journey that allows your God-given potentials to be released so that they can germinate, take root, and be nurtured to maturity. You are likely to find the planning period (the cracking and germinating phase) to be most challenging in your journey to success. Comparably, the planning phase is your hibernating phase when people may not understand you. During the hibernating stage, those that are not with you 'underneath' will not comprehend what is happening in your life. It is the time when you can expect many discouraging comments and indifference from those that misjudge you. It is when you are doing so much but see little progress. It is the phase when many who do not have the resilience to keep pushing downward, into self-searching and upward into available opportunities, will give up. It is a phase at which many will abandon their embryo of success to die.

Success is not a one-time event; it is a process. You have to be ready to undertake the process of planting, nurturing and maintaining your success. You have to be prepared to face the phase of being invisible; when you are 'buried' doing the things that no one but only you can notice. You cannot build success unless you are willing and happy to engage in doing the tough things that release your abilities. If you desire outstanding success, you must grow your own brand.

The embryo of success

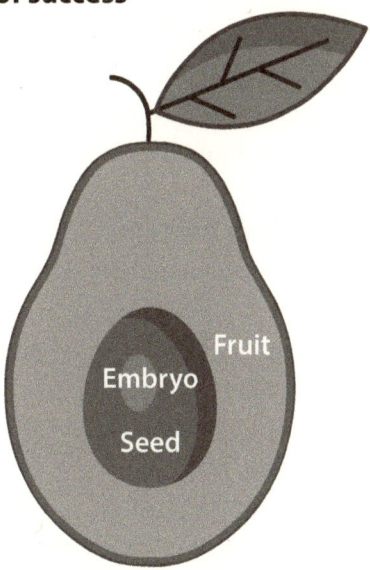

(Copyright © Esther Mburani, 2021)

While you are born with the embryo of success, this embryo can never amount to anything unless you are willing to go through the cracking process. When you stretch yourself open, your embryo of success gets released from its cage and starts to sprout, grow, and blossom into rewarding success.

The cracking process starts at an early age in your life. The process of building your success begins as early as when you are still in your mother's womb. However, at that stage, someone else and not you is in charge. Therefore, we shall skip that stage and focus on when you start to be responsible for building your success. This is when you start school, probably at the age of four or five years. This is when the cracking process begins and continues throughout a lifetime. Since the seed of success must be perpetually planted, cracking is not a one-time experience; it continues throughout life. For instance, Sir Tom Moore subjected himself to the cracking process when he, at ninety-nine years old, challenged himself to walk 100 laps in his garden. That allowed him to release the new embryo of success, and the results were both unprecedented and tremendous.

Cracking and education processes

The absence of or limited education does not imply that one will be unsuccessful in life. Neither does the attainment of education guarantee success. There is a proven record of people who were considered academic failures or never had the opportunity to attain school education but achieved immense success. However, while academic achievement is not everything, it significantly impacts how you are likely to succeed in life. Education is one of the factors that create the existing social structures and social classes. While there are alternative ways to achieve success, education remains the most viable route for many. Education allows students to fix themselves either in the top, middle or bottom class in the society depending on how they are willing to push themselves.

However, education as a stand-alone may not be enough to transform you into becoming a successful person. This is because education is fundamentally different from wisdom. It is possible to be educated and remain unwise and unsuccessful. Therefore, meaningful and transforming education that will enable you to become a successful person must have its foundation on wisdom. In fact, several highly educated people may be deficient in success when it comes to other aspects of life. Therefore, education may not be a conclusive measure of success. But nevertheless, it does substantially contribute towards its attainment in various ways. This is why education is looked at as an investment, and people will spend a fortune to attain it.

While people attend school to invest in their future success, this goal gets lost when one misses the dynamics of how education creates success. Going through the education system is not enough to make you succeed. You may be like the many who do not want to hear this, but the quality of what you achieve in school significantly impacts who you become. This is where the *cracking* becomes relevant in pursuing education. The harder you push yourself into achieving the best possible in your education, the closer you get to your dream.

While you may initially display low abilities, that does not mean that you cannot fly. Any bird that continuously stretches and exercise its wings will at some point fly. While it is true that students exhibit varying potentials, categorization and stereotyping can clip the 'slow charging students' of their wings before they learn how to fly.

Many schools operate learning structures that allow students to sort themselves into the class they are likely to belong to in the future. This is how self-sorting works. While all the students may be in the same class, their work is categorised according to Challenge one, Challenge two and Challenge three. Children are given a choice to attempt the challenge they are comfortable with. Children who do not understand that working hard on their education is a part of the hibernating phase in building their success will be happy to keep doing the easiest. However, students who understand education to be a part of their success building process may start with challenge one but work towards pushing themselves to higher challenges.

It is crucial to understand the negatives of pigeonholing students by the so-called learning abilities. Such categorization may overlook potential. Yet, all children have potential within them. The difference is, for some, it is on the top, while for others, it is placed deep within and may require time and patience to dig out. But the fact is that they all have potential.

While the motive may be genuine in allowing students to attempt challenges that they are comfortable with, the same may hinder them from flying. Stereotyping may make students give up aspiring higher than they are placed. Placing a student on a table classified as a weak or struggling students table may only make him worse. Asking a student to take his lessons with a lower class is likely to sabotage his capacity to aim higher. The logic is simple; you cannot make a student perform better by asking him to aim lower. Nobody progresses by driving in reverse gear. Anybody that wants to advance engages the forward driving gear. When you move a student to a lower table or lower class, you drive them in reverse. Nothing makes progress by growing backwards. There must be a forward progression for anything to grow, be it human beings, animals or plants. So, it is with education. A student may not achieve much if the only strategy used is to give him work that is below his expected academic growth level.

A teaching model where students are placed in groups according to displayed abilities can be crippling to students with hibernating potentials. This can clip your little eagle's wings and turn him into a chicken that only feeds from what is on the ground instead of hunting from the skies. While eagles are known to be masters of the sky, every eagle that can soar knows how challenging it was when it was first dropped by its parents. The parent eagle is not scared to challenge its little one because that is the only way to succeed in life. Likewise, your child can only succeed by being encouraged to face challenging academic tasks rather than being shielded. The earlier your child learns to face challenges, including academic challenges, the more he is likely to succeed in life. A child should not be trained to retreat from problems or seek lower goals because his first or second attempt to reach the highest goal possible has not been successful. You need to focus on imbuing in your child the spirit of resilience from the earliest stage in life. Allow him to know that it is okay to face a hard challenge and fail. If he fails the first time, that is okay as long as he attempts again.

Let your child be comfortable with failing as many times as it takes for him to succeed. People who attempt and fail and keep attempting and failing but never stop attempting are the ones that turn out to be successful. On the other hand, failures are those that attempt, fail and quit. Every mind that is pushed to reach its potential yield positive results. Students who are willing to crack themselves by doing the most demanding challenges allow the embryo in their lives to start sprouting in preparation for more significant future success. What we all know is that students learn differently, but they all can learn. Therefore, instead of lowering the standard, a different approach should be sought to enable your child to learn without dropping the bar at which he is to achieve.

Otherwise, without your being aware, the education system may be preparing your child to be a failure in life. A student that has gone through the education system complying with being given basic assignments may find no motivation to aspiring higher in the working world. As an adult, he may have the mentality of 'any job will do' and be satisfied to operate at the lower level of employees. Instead of standing up to challenges and finding solutions, he may keep changing every job that poses a problem. This will be because he was trained to avoid challenges from his early school years rather than face them and find ways to overcome them. The same self-sorting system is reflected in the grades that are awarded in school. Many schools use the grading system below to rate their students.

A= above age expectation

B= meeting age expectation

C= below age expectation

D= significantly below age expectation

The level at which one achieves in school has a high probability of fitting them into traditional social classes. Those who consistently perform at the 'A' level are likely to settle into the elite class. The ones that achieve between 'A' and 'B' level may join the middle-class tier. Those that are comfortable and satisfied with 'C' and 'D' grades may come to settle in the low class.

Apart from being graded for attainment, students are also graded for their attitude and effort towards their studies. Student's efforts and attitudes are classified in the following manner.

1=Excellent/Highly motivated

2=Good/Consistent

3= Satisfactory/Some inconsistency

4=Poor/Inconsistent

The grading system looks at the student's ability to achieve and attitude towards learning. An average student who gets an 'A' in attitude towards learning may achieve massive success in life. Many achievers were not necessarily 'A' students but average students with an A-plus attitude towards learning and life.

Be it that you are a student in an institution or a student of life, you need to know that at any moment, you are either building success or accumulating failure. You do not start working for success in high school, at the university or when you are employed. The journey starts much earlier than that. This is why every student must cooperate by making himself teachable and doing all it takes to unleash his potential. Without the student's willingness to crack the potential within, a teacher cannot do much. Every student must take up personal responsibility for his success other than thinking that it is the teacher's or parent's duty to make him succeed.

Cracking and career

While it is popularly thought that you are likely to excel when you start with a good job, that may not be necessarily the case. The critical factor that will determine where you end is your attitude and your input in the job. Those are the two key aspects that push people into working classes they eventually end in.

This is why two managers will be employed in the same organization, at the same time and with the same job descriptions but end in different ranks. Ten years down the road, one will have risen to become the CEO while the other remains at the same level that he started. The difference will be in the willingness to handle the cracking process. The manager who ends up as a CEO will have been operating at the *'above expectation'* level. The manager that remains at the same rank will have been comfortable performing at the *'meeting expectation'* level. What will have hindered the manager who remains at the initial position is his fear to face the cracking process. His dislike to push himself into discomfort areas denies the embryo of success within him the opportunity to grow. Nobody reaches the top and stays there without the ability to do the extras.

Only you can create your dream career. While many people may know the career that would be most rewarding to them, few are engaged in making their dream careers. Irrespective of the awareness and the superb knowledge they have, they remain stuck for years doing the old things they do not like, do not enjoy and are less rewarding. What will hold you from attaining your dream career is the fear to undergo the cracking process to unleash the potential that remains trapped within you.

If you consistently feel that there is something that you can do better and enjoy doing than what you are currently engaged in, take that for a signal to change. When you stop ignoring the cry to succeed within you, you embark on the journey to unimaginable success. The embryo of success within you never stops crying out. When you consistently ignore and suppress the cry, you limit your opportunities to achieve higher. The alternatives you seek can never give you the satisfaction of the success you were created to achieve.

The people that enjoy their careers do so because they dared to drop the *'mask jobs'* and allowed themselves to grow irrespective of the challenges that they knew they would face. To build your dream career, you must be prepared to undergo the cracking process by meeting the challenges involved. You should be willing to persistently engage in hard work. Your levels of resilience should be extraordinarily high. You must be ready to face hard choices and make the right decisions. You must make perseverance your constant companion. Your decisions must be governed by principle and not emotions. You must live your days by prioritizing and be willing to make sacrifices. It will be impossible for you to sustainably grow a rewarding and successful career without moving out of your comfort zone.

Cracking in the marriage relationship

Your ability to enjoy your marriage will depend on your willingness to crack. The cracking process will make it possible for you to grow a new self that creates room for your spouse. While it is often mentioned that two married people become one, rarely do people take time to think about the more profound implications. Oneness in marriage involves synchronizing your life with your other half making it possible to enjoy being part of your spouse's life without losing your identity as a person.

'Do two walk together unless they have agreed to do so?' [26]

Marriage is a journey where you need to agree with your spouse to keep the relationship exciting and alive. In marriage, agreeing is two-faced. A couple can agree by sharing the same opinion or agree by consenting to have varying opinions. To agree in marriage means to maintain harmony. To live in harmony with your spouse, you need to push your old bad habits out of your life. However, abandoning old habits is never easy. It will necessitate moving from your comfort zone. You need to take actions to make things work even when you may not feel like doing it. Marriage is not about you having your way. Most of it is about willingly doing what it takes to make your spouse feel loved, accepted and a part of you.

Your marriage union is most threatened when you are going through crisis moments. It is tempting to let go when you feel that your marriage's reality does not match your expectations. Going through and above the numerous challenges in your marriage will remain an impossible task unless you are willing to embrace intricate changes in your life.

To achieve that will require some level of cracking your old self so that your old habits and interests drop out. You may initially resent doing the things that take away your comfort but make your spouse happy. However, if you keep on doing them, they will turn into habits, and if you never stop doing them, they will convert into your new character. The new character you acquire will cause your spouse to be happy. Since happiness is highly contagious, you are likely to share in their joy when you live with a happy spouse. Therefore, your willingness to crack the old habits out of your life creates room for you to develop a character that supports your marriage. When you have a stable and happy marriage, you are more likely to achieve success in other aspects of your life than someone living in a turbulent relationship. A happy marriage can be massive support in your journey to success. However, an unhappy marriage can be extremely draining, leaving you with little energy to invest in other areas of your life.

The usefulness of cracking in parenting

Parenting for excellence requires that you invest a lot of your quality and valuable time into moulding your children into what they were created to be. It also involves taking time to observe the type of embryo of success in your child to create an environment that supports its cracking and sprouting. However, diligence needs to be exercised to avoid the mistake of cracking the child instead of the seed. When you crack the child, he feels crushed. But when you help him to crack the seed, he feels empowered. This makes parenting very delicate, engaging and involving responsibility. It puts you on duty all the time. Authentic parenting involves living and demonstrating that which you desire your children to be.

Becoming an effective parent requires undergoing the cracking process so that your personal interest gives way to the broader importance of nurturing your children. You will have to stop doing some things even when you like them for the sake of setting an example for your children. It may also be necessary that you begin doing some things even though you do not enjoy them, but you will do them for the sake of your children. For example, you may not like exercising, but if you want your children to be physically fit, you will start jogging so that your children can pick the habit from you. If you desire your child to have good health, you will stop smoking so that your child does not pick the deadly habit. To turn your son into a gentleman, you must demonstrate a gentleman's character for him. If you desire your daughter to grow up as a lady, you need to live your life as a lady so that she can learn from you. If you want your children to be good Christians, you need to be a good disciple of Jesus so that they can learn by beholding your life. If your desire for your children is that they succeed, you need to demonstrate success in your life. This means that parenting is not only about providing the things that your children need but providing your experience as an example of what they should be.

You can say that you are a successful parent if you are comfortable and happy with your children becoming what you are. What you are, refers to the values and principles you stand for and demonstrate in your life. When you impart the correct principles and values to your children, you will have bequeathed enough resources to generate their own success. On the other hand, your inability to demonstrate the success you desire for your children will result in generations that struggle to understand real success.

Cracking and personal goals

While the need for personal goals is often emphasized, many people's problem is not about goal setting. In fact, on each first day of January, millions of people set goals that never make it to the next month. The reason people fail is not the absence of goal as it is to the lack of the stamina to undergo the cracking that it requires for them to achieve the goals they have set. The discipline to stick to your goals even when the going gets tough is what you require to set you apart from quitters, mediocres and failures. Goal setting alone is not enough to change your situation. In fact, you can have a great goal, and your situation ends up getting worse instead of getting better. For example, it is possible to set a goal of achieving your ideal body weight within twelve months and instead end up with more weight if you do not do what it takes. The point is, you cannot achieve your goal of attaining an ideal body weight without subjecting yourself to the cracking process.

In this case, the cracking process will involve practicing self-discipline that will enable you to resist the old habits that led you to gain weight. For example, you will be conscious of the type of food you eat and how much you eat. You may not like the kind of food that will help you cut the weight, but this is where your self-discipline will come in; despite your craving for a chocolate cake, you will pick an apple. After a busy day, you may prefer to rush home, have a cup of tea, and watch your favourite TV soap. However, this is where you will need to push yourself into making the right choice. Instead of driving straight home, you will feed in your satellite navigation a new route that takes you home via the gym. Reaching your ideal weight will also mean that you will have to make sacrifices. For example, spending one hour in the gym may require you to give up watching your favourite TV soap.

Success requires making trade-offs by dropping things that stand in your way to realizing your goals and replacing them with the things that enhance your abilities. It is the pain, the sacrifice, the self-discipline, the push, and the discomfort, among other things, that make many give up on their goals. Those who dare to undergo the cracking get rewarded by joining the club of achievers. While everyone can join this club, it remains exclusive because few people are willing to experience what it takes to become a member.

Cracking and attaining good health

Very few people will look at success in terms of good health. Yet good health and life are the fundamental prerequisites you need to operate and attain success in other aspects of life. For instance, you will find that most people will treat their cars with more care than they do their health. Your life is much more precious than your car. You would benefit a lot from it if you treated it better than you treat your car, or at least give it the same attention. For instance, if you are driving and notice a warning light on the dashboard, you will fix it or go to the garage, depending on what the problem is.

On the contrary, you are likely to keep your foot on the accelerating peddle even when your life dashboard is flickering with warning lights. Even when diabetes, heart diseases, obesity, cancer, kidney diseases, arthralgia and liver diseases flash amber lights, you ignore everything. You keep your foot on the accelerating peddle by continuing to do the things you know to be wrong and detrimental to your health and dismissing to do the right things. Even when you know that what you are doing is hurting your health, you do not stop because you enjoy those things. It is absurd to see how many people choose to keep the habits and lifestyle they know to be detrimental to their health. Some will eat the wrong food, take bad drinks, maintain a poor lifestyle and then have medication to rectify the self-caused damage.

On the contrary, most people will panic when they put the wrong fuel in their car because they know it will damage the engine. But when it comes to their bodies, anything goes. The point is, just as it is with your car, every wrong thing that you put in your body causes damage. The damage may be immediate or gradual, but with time it may be irreversible. For instance, even though you love wine, you cannot pour it into your car engine because the mechanic tells you that it will damage the engine. Even though you love the smell of cigarette, you cannot light one and push into your car's exhaust pipe because you know that it will be disastrous. So why put wrong stuff into your body when the doctor tells you that it will damage your health? Common sense?

Sugar, salt, fatty foods, processed foods, alcohol, tobacco, meat, recreational drugs, lack of rest, inadequate access to fresh air and sunshine and many more all gradually but surely blow up your life's engine. Many people know what is bad, but they do not believe that they have the power to quit. That is where the concept of cracking comes in. You can drop all the bad lifestyle habits that destroy your health and replace them with good lifestyle habits.

Cracking is a prerequisite to attaining good health. Many people long for good health, but only those willing to crack the bad habits that are detrimental to their lives can achieve it. Numerous ailments are caused by the sufferer's unwillingness to crack the bad habits out of their lives. The reluctance, indifference, and disinterest to make choices beneficial to one's health have led many to live with excruciating pains and even face premature death. For instance, a person who refuses to give up smoking may at some point have to face lung cancer. A fellow who takes pleasure in junk food may soon have issues with his weight which can become an open gate for other health problems to take root. Folks who find pleasure in drinking alcohol are likely to deal with some heart diseases besides having issues with the liver at some point.

It is ironic and absurd to see many people who would rather suffer and possibly go to their graves prematurely rather than give up the slowly destroying habits. The usefulness of the cracking concept is that it helps you see the reality of the benefit of pushing bad habits, lifestyle and practices out of your life. Good health is a result of intentional choices and pushing yourself to do the right things.

Nurturing your personal tree of success

After the cracking process has enabled the embryo of success to break from its cage and sprout, you get launched to the second stage of attaining your success. At this point, you become aware of your potentials, and you wake up to the pleasant reality that you can change your life. However, you soon realize that awareness alone is not enough to take you to where you want to be. This will start you into the thinking process to assemble the most basic but critical things you need to progress in your journey to success.

I have put together the personal tree of success as a model to demonstrate that you can attain success by using the resources within you. The model's objective is to trigger your realization of the inexhaustible resources and endowments that you have. The purpose of including this section in the book is to let you know that you do not have to wait for tomorrow or wait for that bank loan. Or wait to complete your PhD. You can begin from where you are using the resources that are within you. You will notice that character is the most prominent resource on the tree of success model.

Using a tree's reality, the model gives you a simple but inspiring visual picture of what you need to achieve. While many people get discouraged by their situation and think that success is out of their reach, the personal tree of success will enable you to confront and demystify this fear. When you grasp the logic behind the personal tree of success, you will realize that you have more than ninety percent of what you need to succeed.

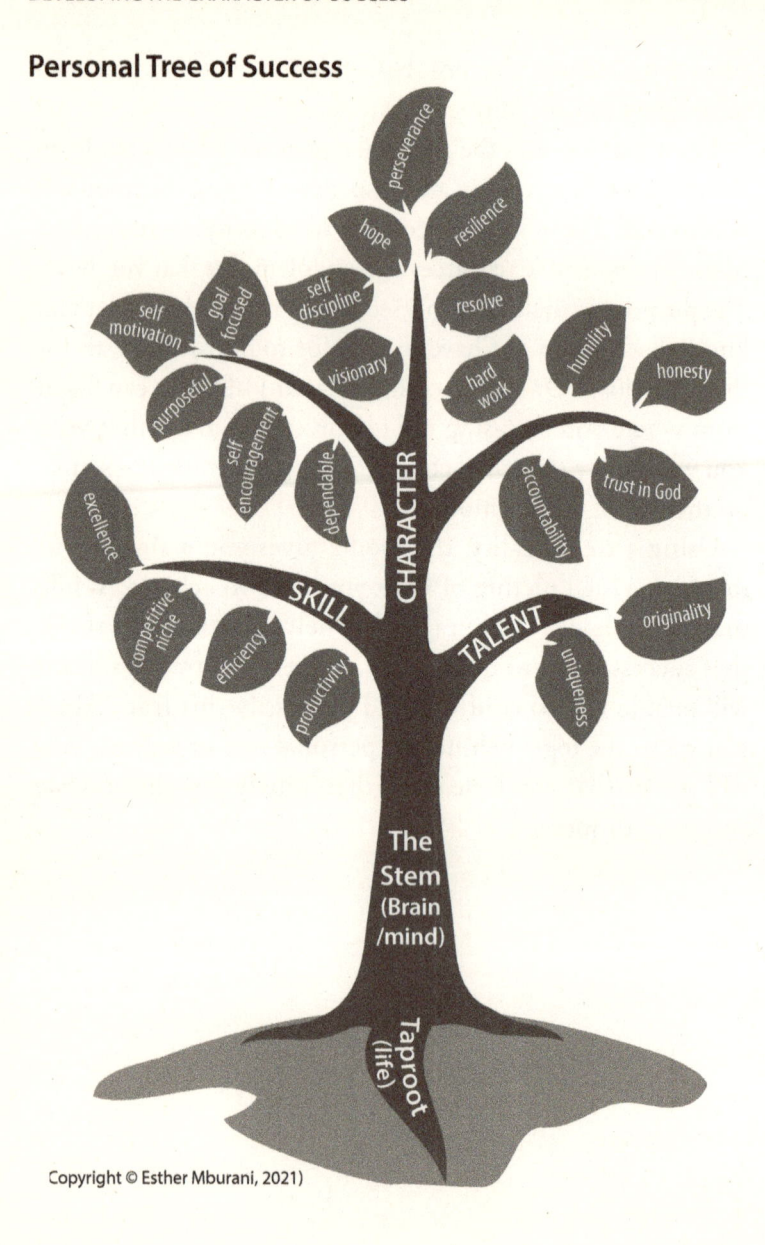

Personal Tree of Success

Copyright © Esther Mburani, 2021)

The key features of the personal tree of success are the taproot, the stem, the branches and the fruits. These are the four critical pillars that you need to succeed. What is fantastic about the personal tree of success is that it brings your attention to some success factors that your professor may never have mentioned. While at the same time deliberately ignoring factors that are usually emphasized by many experts.

While the traditional approach to success seems to favour the concept that those who have, gain more, the personal tree of success model suggests that anybody who bothers to apply the model can succeed. This will be irrespective of their beginning point. According to this model, you do not need to have factors of production such as capital to embark on your success journey. All that you need to start on your journey to success are the following four pillars.

Pillar one: taproot (life)

The taproot on the personal tree of success symbolizes life. The first and most critical resource that you need to achieve success is your life. The use of external aids and support does not make you less competent in terms of achieving success. Even in situations where these are not accessible, you can still get on top of your physical uniqueness and achieve. Your physical challenges do not impair your capacity to succeed. This is why Sir Tom Moore managed to use a walker's support to make those one hundred steps that launched him as a global icon of success.

In the same spirit, Helen Keller, who lost her sight and speech at nineteen months, lived a life that positively changed the world. Her being deaf and blind did not stand in her way to achieving the highest level of success that she was created to achieve. With the support of her brilliant teacher Ms Anne Sullivan, she was able to crack the embryo of success that had been trapped inside her by deafness and blindness. Once her sprout of success was out, she nurtured it into a tree that yielded the fruits that led to her outstanding achievement. Resilience, resolve, hard work, self-encouragement, optimism, self-motivation, and focus were fruits that enabled her to change her life and impact the world. She stretched herself to achieve when she graduated Cum Laude. She became a respected author and lecturer among her other many achievements.

The world is dotted with outstanding people who defied the physical challenges in their lives and went on to use their lives as an incredible resource to become outstandingly successful. Nicholas James Vujicic could not allow his lack of some of the body limbs to suffocate his potentials. His success has been outstanding. He has used his life to inspire millions to know that success is not what you have outside but what lies within you. His character traits of courage, resolve, determination, and self-confidence, among others, enabled him to succeed despite the many odds in his life. Nicholas has demonstrated the fundamental truth regarding success: what matters is one's spirit and not the body one is in. Therefore, if you have life, you have the license to operate on the street of success. With this resource, you can achieve anything.

Pillar two: the stem (your brain and the mind)

The stem on your personal tree of success symbolizes your brain and your mind. The stem supplies nutrients and water to the tree. In the same manner, your mind supplies you with ideas that you convert into success. While the brain and the mind may be distinct aspects of your being, they do work as a team. When using your tree of success model to plan your success, your brain/mind can be perceived as your gold reserves. Your mind is filled with precious gems that you need to excavate.

What you need to become successful is an authentic idea transformable into a relevant and desperately needed reality. Your mind is filled with ideas that are worth millions of pounds. You only need to know how to excavate and package them to meet other people's pressing needs, interests, and aspirations. People who attain success from scratch are those who recognise the worth and power of a good idea. They pick it up and build their success empire on it. The test of a successful idea is not in its sophistication or the amount of initial support and popularity it gets when you first share it with other people. A great idea may be ridiculed and rejected when you share it with those who don't understand your vision and how it will work. To turn an idea into tangible success, you need to be convinced about it and have the capacity to see the end product before you paint your picture.

While many people think that they need to see a consultant for help before starting a new project, the consultant does not really add much to what is already in you. When you sit in the consultant's office after paying a hefty amount in his account, all he does is ask a few questions that trigger you on a thinking process. You can avoid unnecessary expenses of paying someone and ending up solving your own problems. When you free your mind from the common spectrum of thinking, it will effortlessly generate mind-blowing ideas that will launch you to success. When you adopt the habit of engaging in thinking as an activity of success, you will realize that invaluable insights come when your mind is allowed the freedom to roam.

While your physical body may have various limitations, your mind can navigate past your physical challenges and thrust you to an outstanding level of success. Although many tend to think that physical ability is key to attaining success, the personal tree of success model presents a different argument. The model suggests that once you have life and brain/mind, you have the foundation of what you require to attain success. While physical disabilities may present challenges as you pursue success, they cannot stop you from achieving.

This was most demonstrated in the life of Stephen Hawking. Despite his severe physical limitation, he possessed one of the most extraordinary minds in the world of science. His being paralysed, confined in a wheelchair, and losing speech did not hinder him from making substantial research contributions. His life proved that the mind can still be highly productive even when housed in a feeble and disease-battered body.

Pillar three: the branches (talent, character, skill)

Your personal tree of success will have three major branches. The first branch represents talent, the second branch represents character, and the third branch represents skill. When you have life, a functioning brain/mind, relevant talent, the right character and required skill, you have everything necessary to succeed. You will also note that character contributes substantially to your success more than talent and skill.

Pillar four: the fruits

There is a direct link between your personal tree of success and the cracking process we looked at earlier. The sprouting embryo will grow into your tree of success. When well nurtured, your tree will bear fruits on each of the three branches. The talent branch will produce two fruits which are uniqueness and originality. To succeed, you need to present to the world a product that is unique and original. The skills branch will bear four fruits: excellency, efficiency, high productivity and competitive niche. You need these to exist and thrive in a competitive world. The character branch will produce sixteen fruits. Namely, accountability, trust in God, honesty, humility, hard work, resolve, resilience, perseverance, self-discipline, hope, vision, goal-focused, self-motivation, purposeful, self-encouraging and dependability. You can never fail to succeed when you have the above character traits and actively use them. You need these fruits to successfully engage and prevail in any venture. Whether you are an entrepreneur or employee, possessing the above-mentioned character traits will enable you to perform at the 'above expectation' mark. That will allow you to be a class above others and keep you in the lead.

As you can see, the character branch yields the most fruits on your tree of success. The implication is that while you may possess talent and skill, it will be impossible to attain sustainable success without having and maintaining the right character.

Your character is the most rewarding asset that you have. It is the only resource that will continue to earn for you without getting diminished. Your character has the capacity to continuously increase your net value without the input of third parties.

Character is the ultimate legacy that you bequeath to posterity.

Most people's failure is not due to lack of resources as much as it is due to inadequate character. The major contributing factor to your success will be how your character empowers you to relate to challenges, opportunities, resources, and people. To reach your goal of success, you must add value to yourself and spend yourself profitably. Your life is not an inexhaustible resource. Therefore, if you misspend yourself, you will soon be overspent.

Chapter six

The power of rejection

Tapping into the positive power of rejection

Most people dread being rejected. Several people spend a lifetime trying to earn acceptance from the people who will never fully accept them. Dreading rejection can make you spend your entire life being a slave of 'acceptance seeking.' However, you can never succeed unless you are ready and willing to embrace rejection at every stage in life.

Suppose you desire to achieve; you need to learn to look for positives in rejection and use the would-be negative situations to your advantage. Rejection can be experienced at a very early stage and continues throughout life. Therefore, you can only win if you stop fighting it and instead focus on taking advantage of the situations it creates.

I remember when I took our one-year-old to a playgroup, she had to face this challenge for the first time in her life. I brought her in when the other toddlers had formed their circle of friendship. Though I encouraged our daughter to smile and say hello, her efforts were met with coldness. I could see that insisting that our daughter joins would stress her and probably make the other kids solidify their rejection. So, what I did, I smiled at the children who did not want their circle to be interrupted. The purpose was to make our daughter realize that she does not have to be offended if people show that she is not welcome.

The play area was large enough, with many play stations and exciting toys. I encouraged our daughter to try some of the play stations, and soon she was having a good time. She was running to and from with excitement bringing toys to me. Interestingly, when the other kids saw that she was having fun, they stopped what they were doing and joined her.

Rejection has two-sided effects. It can either thrust you to unlimited heights or push you into a bottomless pit. How you get affected will be determined by your attitude and reaction when you encounter it. To benefit, you must keep your emotions in balance and focus on aspects that put you in a better situation that outweighs the rejection. I will use a case to illustrate this point:

CASE ILLUSTRATION EIGHT: JOSHUA

From the time he was enrolled in primary school, his teachers noted that Joshua was an extra brilliant child. He quickly grasped concepts and was always ahead of his classmates. He was made to skip a class because his being ahead of everyone else made it hard to teach the rest. Therefore, the teacher thought sending him on a higher level would give him challenging work to keep him busy. He went through primary and secondary school, being the best in class.

His outstanding academic performance earned him a scholarship. He soon found himself walking on the campus of one of the world's most prestigious universities. By being enrolled in this university, he knew that he had made it to academics' pinnacle. While he should have been the happiest young man on earth, one thing was not right. He realized that his skin colour was different. Much as he could see that he was unique, he quickly noticed that he was an unwanted shade. In fact, his tint disturbed the symmetric flow of the dominant colour.

The message he received from his classmates and professors was, 'This is not your place.' However, instead of allowing this silent rejection to put him out of balance, Joshua decided to use it to his advantage. He thought that if people thought that his skin colour disqualified him from being on the campus, he would prove them wrong. He worked hard and graduated Cum Laude. That gave him an automatic pass to enrol for Masters and PhD degrees which he pursued concurrently. He became a professor, and his presence in that capacity encouraged many students of varying colour to get enrolled.

When taken with a positive attitude, rejection can widen your sphere of operation. While Joshua's initial purpose was to obtain a bachelor's degree and return to his home country, this was drastically changed by the rejection he faced. The power of rejection triggered him to aim higher and put him at a level where he could cause positive changes that were a blessing to many other people. Rejection turned inside-out equals motivation.

To break the shackles that people who reject you try to bind you with, you must have the ability to use that rejection to push yourself higher than they thought you can reach. You do not do that to prove wrong the people who rejected you but protect and preserve your self-worth. However, when mishandled, rejection can be very damaging. It can crush your self-esteem, erase your identity, make you a bitter and reactionary person and destroy your motivation to achieve great things.

When looked at with positive lenses, rejection can become an invaluable asset to you. If you face rejection with the attitude of benefiting from it, it is a valuable tool in illuminating your blind spots. Some things you may never have known that you could do until rejection threw the challenge into your face. Likewise, there are some undesirable things that you may have carried around until the person that rejected you made you realize how these aspects are huge repellents. Either way, if you take decisive action in addressing issues that lie in your blind spot, you are likely to come out as a more successful person.

To protect yourself from becoming a victim of rejection, you need to edit negativity out of your life. Whether faced in the home, at work, in the community or on the street, rejection can be the very force that propels you to success. Here is how you can use your mindset to achieve in situations where you face rejection.

1. **Start with what you have:** Rejection tends to show up at the moment when you need support. It could be that you need capital from the bank, and your loan application gets rejected. That should never be a reason to throw away or abandon your dream. You can reshape your vision and start with what you have. As it was highlighted in the personal tree of success, your mind is your gold mine. If the bank refuses to offer you a loan, go back and dig deeper into your mind. Generate ideas that will enable you to achieve without that loan from the bank. It could be that you are one of the millions losing their jobs due to the effects of COVID-19. Seeing that you are among those that are asked to leave the

company can make you feel rejected. However, look at your situation in a positive way. It can be your turning point to building a more satisfying career for yourself.

2. **Create your own experience:** It is interesting to note how short human memory is. The person sitting behind the desk telling you that he cannot employ you because of lack of experience was also at the beginning of his career without experience. That should cause you to use your mind to think. If he at one time was like you, or even worse than you, and he is now sitting in that seat, that should cause you to realize that you too can reach where you want to be. Therefore, if he does not offer you the job, walk out confidently and go to start creating your own irrefutable experience. I will give an example to illustrate this point.

In 2002, Adam Deering, who was twenty-one-years-old at the time, had his £10,000 loan application to start a debt management company rejected by the bank on the grounds that he was too young and inexperienced. Mr Deering refused to allow the rejection to rob him of his dream. He used the little money; the only money he had to rent a small room which he used as an office to start his debt management business. However, Adam could not manage to buy a desk and a chair. So he sat on the floor of his office and made cold calls. With time, Mr Deering transformed the small business that he started without capital, without an office chair and an office desk, into a multimillion-pound business. After seventeen years, at the age of thirty-nine, Mr Deering bought the very bank building where he was refused a loan of £10,000 at the price of £450,000.

The point is, when you know where you are going, lack of experience can never hinder you from progressing to your destination.

3. **Know that there is always an alternative:** Rejection will lose its power over you if you approach situations with a mindset that is open to other options. There is never one solution, one job, one offer. People that want to victimize you through rejection will manipulate your mind by crippling your ability to think about alternatives. As long as you know that there are other options, other ways of doing things, rejection will not deter you from achieving.

4. **Know that it is okay to do things for the first time:** Trying to eliminate the *'first'* is an attempt to alter nature. There will always be that first interview, that first job, that first business, that first relationship, that first meeting and that first book. In short, there is a first to every aspect of life. The sooner you get at peace with that reality, the more likely you will score high achievements in the things you do for the first time.

5. **Sever your future from your past:** The crippling power of rejection thrives on what happened in the past. To move forward, you must deliberately detach your present and future from the negatives in your past. If your business plan was rejected in the past, it does not mean that your next business plan will not be accepted. If the first publisher rejected your manuscript, it does not mean that your manuscript is unpublishable. If your fiancé left you, it does not mean that you will not fall in love again.

6. **Possess a liberated mind:** If we refer to the personal tree of success again, you will remember that your mind is where the wealth is. Therefore, to succeed, you need to guard your wealth deposit against controllers. When you experience rejection, it can control how you approach life for the rest of your life. A mind that is not *'rejection proofed'* may soon lose its capacity to function.

   However, on the other hand, a mind that is well equipped and prepared thrives amidst rejection and becomes unstoppable. The point is, it is excellent for people to reject you; when that happens, you find your independence to operate in another circle. It is okay for an application to be turned down. When that happens, you get an opportunity to explore the alternatives. It is okay for a friend to reject you and walk away because the room is created for new friendships.

7. **Create your reality:** You must have the ability to believe in yourself before others can believe in you. The reality that is being talked about here is different from being presumptuous or myopic. For example, before you go for that job interview, you need to be convinced that you can do that job better than any other candidates. That conviction will impact how you will behave before, during and after the interview. It will not matter if the panel behind the desk feels differently about you, and they do not offer you the job. You will drive home knowing that you can do a good job. You only need to find the person with the right sight to see that in you.

8. **Magnify positives and minimize the negatives in your life:** The logic behind this is that what you see most of the time is what you will end up believing, working towards, and becoming.

9. **When you encounter rejection, approach life with a new mind:** do not allow rejection to ruin your day or interfere with your plans.

10. **Take time to learn from rejection:** Many service providers thrive and build their success on this principle. When you tell your service provider that you are leaving, they may not try to convince you to stay, but they will want to know your reasons for going. The rationale is for the company to avoid losing more clients for similar reasons. In the same way, knowing why you have received a rejection will enable you to prevent the same situation from re-occurring.

Chapter seven

The disabling power of trying

When you stop trying, you can do anything. The moment your brain receives the command to 'try', it automatically activates the option of giving up. However, when your brain gets the command to 'do', there are no options given. It, therefore, focuses on completing the task. The command to 'do' gives your will the tenacity not to give up. The command to 'do' also empowers your entire being (body, soul, and mind) to work synergistically and achieve what you desire.

Success is guaranteed only when you eliminate the option of giving up. I will use the marriage scenario to illustrate this further. However, before I proceed with this illustration, it is advisable to put your safety first and seek appropriate help if you are in a potentially harmful relationship. That said, here is an example of how the disabling power of trying can affect outcomes.

When your relationship is deteriorating, and you say to yourself that:

'I will give this marriage a chance.'

Your brain will receive a 'try command'. Meaning that your brain will register the need to 'try'. Therefore, if you try and things do not change, you will feel justified to give up because, after all, you have tried. You have met the expectation. After trying, your brain may produce a report that looks like this: 'I have tried to save this marriage, but it is not working.' The problem with the try command is that it does not activate the resolve button. Using the same marriage scenario, if you gave your brain a command that reads like this: 'I must make this marriage work.' Your brain will receive an absolute command. The absolute command automatically activates the resolve button. That will make your brain search engine browse through all possible options on how to save your marriage. Your brain will not stop searching until every option is exhausted. The report that you get may read like this: 'I need to put more time into my marriage, my husband and I need to see a marriage counsellor', and so on. The point is the absolute command to save your marriage puts your brain on the task of looking for various solutions that will meet the expectation of saving your marriage. Therefore, the option of giving up will be eliminated because it will not be registered as part of the expectation. In every hard time that you face, your willpower can only be stretched to the expectation you set.

Several relationships that break up could have been saved had the parties involved approached issues with the right attitudes. You probably know people who had severe problems in their marriage. When everyone thought that the relationship was over, the couple worked out their differences and are now enjoying a blissful marriage. Every marriage has the potential to succeed or fail. It is the command that parties engage in dealing with their marital challenges that, to a great extent, determines whether they save or lose their union.

I do acknowledge that there are unfortunate cases where a

couple will have different resolutions. While you may have resolved to save your marriage, your spouse may be determined to end it. In such a case, you should still have the satisfaction of knowing that you did not give up on your marriage; someone else did. In such a situation, you need to protect yourself against self-blame. If you did what you could to save your marriage, but your spouse was determined to ruin it, do not punish yourself for what was not your fault. Do not allow his schemes of self-justification to portray you as a failure. Do not receive the blame that people who ruined their marriages like to push to their ex-spouses.

Success is not always achieving winning results; there are situations where you will still be successful even when the results are negative. In some cases, victory is at the motive level.

The crippling power of 'trying' on your career

The extent to which you will succeed in your career will depend much more on your mindset than your abilities. Every person that works diligently has the potential to reach the top. When you start a job with the attitude of 'giving it a try,' you may soon find yourself miserable or wanting to quit the job. The very fact that you are approaching a job with an attitude of trying means that you are emotionally not determined to succeed. However, when you start a career with the resolve to succeed, your attitude fortifies your willpower to meet and deal with any challenges. The positive attitude that you possess gives you the tenacity to overcome any difficulties that may be involved. When you approach a task with the resolve to successfully do it, not only do you achieve success, but you also get to enjoy what you are doing. The challenges involved become your targets and milestones of achievements. Therefore, your excitement will continue to heighten as you surmount one challenge after another. It is the ability to celebrate accomplished goals that makes work exciting and keeps you looking forward to another day of work.

While many people will look for so-called good jobs, you need to know that any job can be great or miserable. Irrespective of the number of digits on the paycheque plus other benefits, you can still be miserable if a job is approached with the wrong mindset. With the right mindset, you can turn a lousy job into an exciting and well-paying job. What matters in a career is not where you start but where you aim to end.

Several people get it wrong when they blame either their managers or workmates for their inability to enjoy their work. When you get you right, it will be possible to enjoy and excel in any job. However, when you get you wrong, any job can turn out to be a nightmare. Unless you deal with you, a mere change of employment will never give you the job satisfaction you desire. When you keep writing resignation and application letters, you stand little chance of achieving career success because you deny yourself a fair opportunity to grow.

The reality in the world of career is that there is no easy way to excel. It all comes with dedication, commitment, and hard work. Those who are at the top and seem to be enjoying it is because they worked hard, worked smart and refused to be discouraged when they were on their way to the top. Being at the top cannot make you a happy person if you were grumpy at the bottom. This is because reaching the top does not mean that you will stop working hard. When you stop working hard, the gravity of competition pulls you down.

To succeed sustainably, you must stop looking for encouragement from other people and become your own cheerleader. If you want consistency in motivation, only you can provide it. I will use an illustration to explain this point further.

Natalia was facing a rough time at her workplace because a workmate determined to keep her miserable by consistently finding something to annoy her. She contemplated quitting the job when she talked to me because she could no longer put up with the situation. When I asked her if she had achieved the purpose for which she took the job. Her answer was negative. That helped her realize that the workmate was just an inconvenience on her way to success. So, she decided to ignore him and pursue her purpose in doing this job.

There are three factors that will determine whether you will enjoy or dread your job. The first is; whether you decide to 'try' or 'do' the job. The second is whether you focus on the purpose of doing the job or the situations at your job. The third is whether you focus on you or other people at your place of work.

Changing you versus changing the job

Changing jobs is valid only if done for the right reasons, such as career growth and other professional strategic goals. You may not change the way people behave towards you. But it is within your power to change how you react to their behaviour. As you work and interact with people, you will note that some are hard or even impossible to please. The antidote for avoiding the disappointment of working with mean people is to relate to them with grace. Meaning that you treat them not as they deserve but better than they merit. Without succumbing to abuse or subjecting yourself to being their doormat or punching bag, you learn to offer such people, unconditional love. When you give unconditional love to mean people, it becomes impossible to be offended because you do not expect anything good in return. That will help you not to be bothered by people's attitudes or how they behave.

A shift in your relationships paradigm by stopping to focus on being treated fairly and concentrating on treating others kindly is likely to yield positive results. That can be achieved when you stop operating on the grounds of 'fairness' and relate with people on the level of empathy. To take this route will require more than merely meeting expectations. You will need to have the willingness to walk the extra mile. The reward though simple is priceless. Inner peace is the trophy that you will receive. Offering unconditional love and treating people with grace will keep you out of reach of mean people's behaviour.

You determine how you live your life

You have the choice to be in charge of your life or surrender and let other people and circumstances determine your destiny. The biggest catastrophe is not the disaster that happens in your life but your inability to take charge of your life. To soar above the crisis, you need to resolve not to give up pursuing your desire, irrespective of how challenging the situation might be. While it is okay to acknowledge the temporary discomfort you suffer during a crisis, you need to keep focused on the ultimate achievement that you desire. You should dare spread your wings beyond the familiar horizon and explore the unfamiliar.

People will talk down your plans as being unrealistic.

However, you need to know that your personal plans do not have to make sense to other people. They only need to be logical to you, the executor. You need to have the stamina that cannot be broken by what you are going through. Focus on the end results and not the challenges involved in the process.

Most important, you need to learn to depend on God and trust Him even when there are no visible indicators of how things will work out. Finally, you must learn to practice unwavering faith and appreciate that faith does not depend on tangibles. At times, faith will make you seem to be a lone walker in the journey of life. However, you and God are an excellent team to face any crisis.

Chapter eight

Overcoming crisis

Crisis has been defined as a decisive moment, a time of danger or great difficulty, a turning point, a critical time, or moment. Crisis has also been associated with disaster, emergency, calamity, and catastrophe.[27]

Various authors use different words and phrases to define what crisis is and its meaning. However, irrespective of the definition given, there is one indisputable truth; life does not and cannot remain the same when a crisis hits. Going through a crisis will change you either for the worse or for the better. While many people will believe that when a crisis hits, it leaves you shattered and devastated, it is possible to emerge from a crisis as a better person than you were before.

While any person can be swirled off their feet by a crisis, the fundamental difference between those who get crushed and those who thrive is in the choice of landing. The case of Martha Hancock provides a perfect example of this truth. In June 2021, Martha Hancock, wife of Matt Hancock, the Secretary of State for Health and Social Care of the United Kingdom from 2018-2021, was hit by a double tragedy. Before that moment, Martha had believed that she was happily married to her husband of fifteen years and the father of her three children. However, the crisis hit hard when she, in just one day, graphically discovered that her husband was having an affair, and he told her that their marriage was over. He, within hours, left the family home to huddle with his lover. Composed and dignified, Martha took the crisis in a stride. Shortly after the bombshell, which was so public, Martha was seen calmly walking the family dog. She remained in charge and faced the merciless paparazzi who hunted her down and shoved cameras in her serene face for the crime of being a faithful wife to a cheating husband. Martha's personality sparkled in her moment of crisis. She was deeply and widely admired for her grace, resilience and dignity. Her marriage might have ended, but she was resolved to keep her life going. You can choose to land firm on your feet, or you can resign to whichever position the crisis throws you. Choosing to land on your feet will keep you in charge of your life. In Martha's case, she remained in charge, despite her crisis.

On the other hand, if you allow the crisis to toss you in any direction it wants, you will lose control and become chronically stuck in an unpleasant situation. There is no more pathetic situation than when you give up control of your life to a crisis.

To achieve during a crisis, you must avoid being distracted by the pains you are going through. A crisis cannot be dealt with by applying cosmetic solutions. Things like drugs, alcohol and other tranquillizers have no power to sort you out when you are in a crisis. They can only provide cosmetic respite, but when the cosmetic is washed off, you come face to face with the same problems. Superficial solutions only help to sink you further into the crisis. To pull out of a crisis, you need a sober mind to face and deal with the cause of the calamity, pain and frustration. You need to summon the courage and have the resolve to deal with, manage, remove or soar above the situation.

Preparing for crisis

Some types of crises can be anticipated. Thus, adequate preparations can be made on how to deal with them by being proactive. For example, it is possible to expect that you might be out of a job at one point. Therefore, you will endeavour to proactively make savings that will enable you to cope during the period you will not be employed.

However, even those reasonably anticipated, most crises hit when least expected, thus making the impact of the blow formidable. The suddenness of a crisis may initially make it seem impossible to pull through. For instance, going to your doctor for a routine check is not something you would typically worry about. However, after doing the tests, the doctor may tell you that the results indicate a life-threatening condition and that you may have limited time to live. Nobody will refute the fact that such a crisis hits hard.

However, how you react to the unpleasant news will determine how you will live your life from that point on words. At such a moment, the greatest threat to your life will not be the disease that has been discovered in your body but your reaction to the fact that you have the disease. The effect of a bad reaction can kill you before the disease gets you. On the other hand, the right response can empower your body to fight and defy the impact of the disease and enable you to live longer than predicted by your doctor.

There are situations when life's longevity will not matter as much as how you live the time you have left. When you team up with God, you can face life-threatening situations and still be at peace. When you have the right attitude, you do not stop performing even in a crisis. I was touched by an elderly lady in the church as she faced her final battle with cancer. The frontline was her hospital deathbed. Knowing that she was living her last moments did not deter her from putting up a good fight. She did all she could to share the good news of salvation with everyone who was within her reach. Whenever my husband, who was her pastor, visited her, she asked him to bring more literature that she could give out. She shared the good news of salvation with doctors, nurses, cleaners, porters, and fellow patients. It was clear that she had a goal, and the length of time she had left did not discourage her from achieving more success each day. She rested from her labour, knowing that she had done an excellent job. She waits for the trumpet of the Lord, which will wake her up to eternal life.

'Be anxious for nothing, but in everything by prayer and supplication, with thanksgiving, let your requests be made known to God; and the peace of God, which surpasses all understanding, will guard your hearts and minds through Christ Jesus.' [28]

Antidotes to crisis

Antidote 1. Develop the faith that defies your crisis

Faith defined

According to the dictionary, faith is defined as 'complete trust or confidence, a firm belief especially without logical proof.' [29] This definition is very much in agreement with the meaning given by the Bible of what faith is, which is; 'the substance of things hoped for, the evidence of things not seen.' [30]

Note that the Bible definition of faith as 'evidence of things not seen' relates closely with the dictionary definition of faith being a 'firm belief especially without logical proof.' However, despite the seeming similarity between the dictionary and the Bible definitions of faith, the Bible definition gives something extra, which the dictionary definition does not give. The Bible states that faith is 'evidence', therefore does not need further proof.

The Bible definition of faith may initially appear paradoxical; how can one have evidence of things not seen? Faith makes that which would otherwise be illogical, logical, invisible, visible, and irrational rational. Faith has the capacity to turn a hopeless present into a future full of hope. Faith is the bridge between the present dark reality and the anticipated bright future. Faith is not dependent on circumstances; it makes you stand firm irrespective of your circumstances.

It is impossible to face a crisis and thrive beyond it unless your faith is superior to what is standing in your way. In the context of crisis, faith is that mystical power that enables you to keep afloat when you should be sinking. It is that unique element that supernaturally holds you together when you should be falling apart.

Every person has faith. You, too, have it. It is that power that shapes and directs your life. A person's faith can be in God, a fellow human being, animals, objects, images, material things or power, among many others. Having no faith is also faith. Therefore, the fact that you do not have faith in God does not mean that you do not have faith at all; it instead means that you have put your faith in something else other than God.

However, where you put your faith will influence how you face and handle the crisis that comes into your life. Faith is a transforming power. It changed simple men and women who would have remained in oblivion to become timeless heroines and heroes. When faced with situations that could have crushed and obliterated them, they chose to anchor their lives on faith, and the results were fabulous.

Although you acquire faith before a crisis, its manifestation becomes visible to those around you when there is a crisis. Your faith will qualify as true faith when it becomes the only thing you have to cling on to carry you through a crisis.

CASE ILLUSTRATION NINE: QUEEN ESTHER

Esther is a kind of Cinderella character in the Bible. She is an orphan girl from a captive Jewish family who is raised by her older cousin Mordecai. From an insignificant and unpromising background, she wins the beauty contest to find the new queen to replace Queen Vashti. The latter had been banished by the king. You can read Queen Esther's fascinating life story from the Bible in the book of Esther chapters two to eight.

Born in a poor captive family, living in a foreign land, and orphaned at a tender age, there was nothing much for Esther to look forward to. Even though little girls dream of becoming princesses, they usually put their dreams into perspective when they face their realities. To Esther, her reality was a humble life; her station was destined to be a common Jewish woman living in exile. However, beyond and above her most wild imagination and dreams, by God's providence, Esther finds herself in the king's palace; not as a servant, not as a chambermaid, not as the kings' concubine, but as the queen, the wife of the king whose empire stretched from India to Ethiopia.

Esther's life and that of her fellow Jews was constantly under threat as they lived in exile. Becoming the queen should have offered her assurance that she was out of danger. However, as you may one day realize, you are most tested when you are most blessed. In Esther's case, her very entrance into the king's palace brought her face to face with the same danger she thought to have escaped. At times, the higher God places you, the higher your tests are also likely to be. The crux of Esther's crisis was whether or not to put her own life into danger by attempting to save her people. Esther also faced a crisis of identity. It was a dreaded moment of truth about who she was instead of what the king and the entire kingdom believed she was.

In life, crises will come your way and make you think that you are safe if you hold your peace and let things remain the way they are. There are situations where you will believe that keeping your mouth shut is less risky than speaking out. There are moments when you will think that staying silent is what you must do to save your neck. When you attain the right character, it will push you to do and say the right things even when personal stakes are high. Your decisions will be directed by rightness as opposed to safety. When you are in the middle of a crisis, God will expect you to make choices that clearly show which side you stand on, irrespective of the consequences. There are moments when you cannot sit on the fence anymore. You will encounter situations that will demand a choice.

From the time Queen Esther realized her calling, she became unstoppable in pursuing it. Her actions indicate strong faith that is guided by both courage and wisdom. Queen Esther knew that she had to act irrespective of the danger that roamed over her head. The awareness of the precarious nature of her mission made Esther approach the crisis with a smart plan. Crisis time is a time to act and act appropriately.

The key ingredients in Queen Esther's plan that enable her to achieve success were:

1. The Queen did not dare take a step before seeking God's intervention in her crisis. Instead, she made God the centre of her plan. She did this through fasting and prayer.

2. She solicited for support from the people who cared about her.

3. She approached the crisis with a calm and sober mind.

4. She set the right time and chose the most appropriate environment when to attack her adversary.

Queen Esther approached her crisis and, indeed, the plight of her people with a resolve that could neither be broken nor intimidated by the dangers involved. She very well knew that the controversy was beyond her and her people. She was aware that the battle was between God and the devil, but her life had become the battlefield, in fact, the front line. With this knowledge on her mind, Esther was not only prepared to face the battle but was also ready to die fighting. Her resolve is echoed in the unmatched words of courage ever uttered by a tender queen:

'Go, gather all the Jews who are present in Shushan and fast for me; neither eat nor drink for three days, and I will fast likewise.

And so, I will go to the king which is against the law; and if I perish, I perish!' [31]

To comprehend Queen Esther's crisis, you need to first understand the situation surrounding her. First, the law was that anyone who appeared before the king without being summoned would be put to death. The only exemption was if the king raised his sceptre at the person. Secondly, the king had lost interest in Queen Esther. He had not seen her for thirty days. This implies that the king had no more affection or tender feelings for her. Therefore, Queen Esther was aware that daring to go to the kings' presence would probably give him legitimate reasons to get rid of her forever. Thirdly, Esther, who had just replaced Queen Vashti, knew that the king had no problem getting rid of his queen- no matter how beautiful she may be. She had first-hand knowledge that it did not take the king a second thought to get rid of Queen Vashti, whose beauty was unmatched in the entire kingdom. Therefore, it was common sense for Queen Esther to know that the king would find no problem getting rid of her if she acted in a 'presumptuous' manner.

Therefore, when Queen Esther says, *'...so I will go to the king, which is against the law; and if I perish, I perish'*. She knew that her action could potentially end her life.

Faith will empower you with courage that looks your crisis straight in the face

As Queen Esther approached the great portal leading to the throne room, her probably trembling hands lost the strength to push the giant doors open. She could have felt the need to run back to her chamber and be safe, at least for a while. However, the death sentence that roamed over her people charged her with courage. Instead of retreating, she advanced. By the grave look on her face, not even the king's guards could dare stop her from stepping into the inner court. She stood before the king with the courage of a lioness and the grace of a deer.

The king, who could have probably been attending kingdom matters with his officials, was compelled to bring business to a sudden halt. With awe, he gazed at the previously delicate queen standing opposite the throne room with the courage of a lioness ready to defend her cubs. Her demeanour presented a combination of majesty, courage, and unmatched beauty.

When your life is guided by a noble, selfless motive, no crisis can erode your dignity and self-worth. A noble cause will give you inner confidence that will not depend on how others perceive or regard you. When you ask God to move ahead of you on your journey to success, He walks ahead of you and neutralises perils that lie in your way.

As Queen Esther approached the throne, she respectfully bowed and touched the sceptre in the king's hands. The king was moved, his heart filled with love for his queen; he made an offer that a king would rarely make. This is what he said:

'What do you wish, Queen Esther? What is your request? It shall be given to you up to half of the kingdom'.

It was extraordinary for the king to be willing to give away half of his kingdom and power, especially to a queen who had lost his favour. In your life, there will be moments when God will seemingly leave you to walk the scary path alone. There will be those times when everyone has lost hope about your ability to make it. Some situations will cause you to feel as if you are living your last moments. But, even then, you should keep walking toward your goal. No matter how intimidating, threatening, and hopeless your situation may seem, success will come only if you do not stop walking.

The importance of faith when pursuing success amidst a crisis.

The experience of Queen Esther presents faith lessons that are important in pursuing success amidst a crisis.

(i) Faith makes it possible for you to walk on the path of success even when you are in the middle of a crisis. When you face misfortune, you can take two possible routes: a path that plunges you further into the crisis or a way that walks you out of the crisis. Whether you walk further into the mess or walk out of it will depend on the character you engage as you respond to the situation.

(ii) Faith does not require you to see the end of the journey; you only need to see where to put your next foot and take one step at a time until the journey comes to an end.

(iii) When you have faith, you will step forward in the right direction rather than retreat in the wrong direction. You will keep moving, even when it seems that you are on your last journey.

(iv) Faith will give you the character of courage to confront situations that are humanly intimidating and impossible.

(v) Faith gives you the privilege of moving with God in your struggles to achieve. When you walk in faith, God moves with you.

(vi) Faith will give you confidence and liberate you from the fear of not seeing sense in your situation. This is because actions of faith do not need to be logically sound; they only need to be divinely approved.

(vii) When you have faith, you will acquire a character that appreciates people not because of the rank they hold but because they are human beings. For example, Queen Esther humbles herself by asking her subjects to support her in prayer and fasting.

(viii) Faith will make it possible for you to develop a selfless character by stopping to focus on yourself and work for the common good of those around you.

(ix) Faith will ground your character in trusting God. When you face a crisis with faith, you will know that if God has allowed a situation in your life, He will give you the strength to withstand and even overcome.

(x) Faith will enable you to nurture the character of being content. You will know that whatever God decides to do regarding your situation, His decision is the best. Therefore, you will be willing to trust Him irrespective of the outcome.

(xi) When you face a crisis, you should not be embarrassed to link yourself to a support network of the people who care. Nobody is too strong to need the prayers of other people.

(xii) Faith will save you from feeling stranded in your crisis; you will continue pushing forward even when you cannot see the light and your tunnel seems to be endless. Practical faith is not the ability to see the light at the end of the tunnel but the stamina to keep going even when there is no visible light.

(xiii) Having faith will liberate you from the shackles of peer and societal expectations to conform to popular and politically correct ideas as you pursue your success. Faith will at times require that you swim against the social tide. However, as long as the success path you are taking agrees with God's immutable laws and morality, you do not have to be held back by the opinions of others.

Antidote 2: live for a calling that is bigger than the crisis you face.

Having a calling to live for makes it possible to achieve in crisis. Your life should not stop just because you have been hit by a disaster. You must keep faithful to your calling irrespective of the crisis you are facing. It is by teaming up with God that you can have a calling that defies even death. You can find a lot of satisfaction in a few days lived with God and for the right calling than you did in decades of void life. People with a calling can achieve much on their death beds than people without a calling achieve in a lifetime. If you want to achieve success, you do not wait until the crisis is over. When you find your calling, there will be no obstacle big enough to stop you from advancing. Awareness of your calling will move you to push walls placed in your path to success.

What gave Queen Esther the courage to face the crisis was the realization of her calling. Before understanding the reason why she was in the palace, Queen Esther was timid and susceptible. Even though she saw the calamity that was coming, she felt helpless. In fact, for a while, self-pity numbed Queen Esther's ability to act as she perceived the crisis she and her people were facing as insurmountable. Her helplessness is reflected in the initial response she sent to Mordecai:

'All the king's officials and the people of the royal provinces know that for any man or woman who approaches the king in the inner court without being summoned, the king has but one law: that he be put to death. The only exception to this is for the king to extend the gold sceptre to him and spare his life. But thirty days have passed since I was called to go to the king.'

After Mordecai helped Queen Esther realize her calling, which was her purpose in the palace, she found the courage and resolve to face the crisis. From that point onwards, her fear was replaced with unstoppable courage.

Your success begins the moment you identify your calling. You need to position yourself in a manner that will allow you to be moved by your calling irrespective of the situation you are operating in. People who do not achieve success perceive life as a sequence and live it as a routine. They understand the routine of life as going to school, graduating, getting a job, getting married, having a family, retiring, and end of life. Their achievements do not usually go beyond routine expectations.

However, outstanding success requires a foundation. You make the foundation for your success when you take time off your routine activities and identify a specific reason you want to dedicate yourself. Having a clear calling will give you an edge and keep you moving even in the most challenging situations. Your calling will provide you with the tenacity you need to keep going and not give up even when the situation you face looks bleak. For instance, what makes the medics wake up every morning and walk to the COVID-19 frontline on the wards is not the need to keep their jobs but the calling to preserve and save lives. What moves a nurse to hold the hand of a dying patient and give her comfort is not the pay she expects at the end of the month but the calling to ease human suffering. What pushes a police officer to advance in the direction of gunfire is not the desire for another rank but the calling to protect and save lives.

When everything that gave meaning to your life is gone, the presence of a calling will compel you to relaunch yourself and reclaim your valuable space on earth. In your moments of discouragement, the awareness of your calling will stop you from sinking. When you have explicit knowledge of your calling, you can survive any crisis. When the storms of life blow, your calling will hold you together and keep you from disintegrating.

Benefits of living for a calling that is bigger than the crisis you face.

(1) Living for a significant calling will give you the insights and motivation you need to remain focused even during hard times.

(2) Having a significant calling will enable you to live above prejudice. Your focus will be on what you need to achieve. You will know that your value is not derived from how people perceive you but from what you live for.

(3) A clear calling will make you dare to step where most people are timid to put their feet.

(4) The presence of a calling will enable you to cope with the challenges involved in pursuing your dream. You will know that it is what you stand for that will ultimately count.

(5) When you have a calling, you will not concede to a life of mediocrity.

(6) A calling will help you establish the standard for assessing your success. Irrespective of other people's opinions, you will have a standard to determine your performance.

(7) Your calling will provide a pivot for every achievement in your life.

(8) Your calling will influence the choices you make and the decisions you take during hard times.

(9) Your calling will enable you to perceive your job not as an end in itself but as a means to fulfil your calling.

(10) Living for a calling will give you a worth that is beyond monetary and material possessions. The importance of this is

that even when you incur a loss, you will still have a reason to live for.

(11) Your calling will enable you to manage interruptions. You are likely to encounter several disruptions on your way to success. Examples of these are oppositions, impossibilities, ill health, lack of resources, new opportunities, relationships, disappointments, betrayals, loneliness, and loss.

(12) When you have a calling, you become intentional. Every door you choose to walk through will be strategically selected to resonate with your calling and lead you to higher success.

(13) Your calling will act as your Global Positioning System (GPS). Life is like a network of roads. When you have a calling, it makes it possible to navigate through the maze of options. That will help you avoid wasting time with the unnecessary changing of jobs which usually happens when you are unsure of what you want to do. When you have a calling, you are clear of what you want to do from the onset. When it comes to life choices, all roads do not lead to Rome. A calling will enable you to be intentionally selective. For instance, you will turn down a job offer that diverts you from your calling. However, turning down a job offer when you desperately need an income may sound crazy to many. Only the focused, who know what they want, can do that.

It is crucial to know that failure is every step that takes you away from your big picture. Since you have one life, you cannot afford to run it on bets. It is impossible to leave behind a legacy when you operate your life on the philosophy of 'anything will do'.

(14) When those who do not understand your calling judge you as a failure, the knowledge of your mission will enable you not to be distracted. You will survive criticism by contextualising your choices and maintaining the focus on your calling.

(15) Your calling will motivate you to continue growing. When you are clear about what you want to do and achieve, you will be compelled to keep progressing even when you swim against the tide.

(16) When you have a calling, you will not go after other people's dreams.

(17) Right choices are not necessarily easy and can at times be perceived as unpopular. Critical decisions should never be based on factors such as convenience, popularity or comfort, among others. The litmus test that your choices should be based on should be how they fit in and contribute to your calling. It is more realistic to achieve success if you are focused and know what you want to do. I will give a brief illustration.
My husband and I chatted with a young lady who was about to join the university. During our interaction, we asked her what she was planning to study. We were surprised when she said that she was unsure about the course she wanted to take. She explained that she was considering either social work or law, but she was yet to decide. When we asked her

what she wanted to achieve in life. She did not give a clear answer to that question either. Seeing that she was struggling, we put the question in another way and asked what she was passionate about and could see herself enjoying doing. She still did not put her fingers on anything. Finally, we asked her what she thought would make her both excited and unstoppable. That made her face radiant, and she said with confidence, 'I want to empower people. I want to tell them that they can do it.' She then paused for a moment as if she was lost within her thoughts. Then, in a solemn tone, she whispered: 'I just want to motivate people.' For the rest of the conversation, she was focused, passionate and talked confidently about what she desired to give to the world.

Having a calling to live for will make you original and outstanding in what you do. Moreover, when you mingle with people of exceptional minds, you will realize that they tend to resent 'cut and copy' personalities who parrot other people's inventions. Therefore, if you desire to work with great minds, find your calling and be authentic and original in what you offer to the world.

A calling will help you not to be scared when you do things in your own style. When you live for a valid calling, you will not shy away from being innovative. You will be comfortable doing what no one else is doing as long as it is the right thing to do.

What hinders many people from excelling is because they are timid to do what nobody else is doing. As a result, great ideas are abandoned every day just because nobody has tried them before. The majority of people will feel reluctant or even scared to venture into the unknown. They feel intimidated to take a path that has not been trailed by others. However, a clear calling will empower you to focus on what you want to achieve, irrespective of whether you will be the first and last person to do it.

Antidote 3: Make the right decisions at the appropriate time

To achieve, you do not have to wait until the crisis is over before you can move; you have to dare move in the crisis. When you decide amidst your crisis, it solidifies your resolve to thrive beyond what you are going through. Having a positive attitude in hard times will enable you to navigate an unpleasant situation. The right decision taken during a crisis will increase your abilities to cope and minimise the chances of being crushed by what you are going through. I will use an illustration to explain.

CASE ILLUSTRATION TEN: AMELIA

Amelia received a text message from her boyfriend telling her that he was ending their relationship. She was shocked by the text because, according to her, their relationship was good. In fact, she expected him to upgrade it by proposing marriage to her. However, since she could not believe what she was reading, she decided to call her boyfriend and determine what was happening.

The phone rang several times before her boyfriend could pick it. When he finally did, his voice sounded very indifferent. That seemed unusual to Amelia, who was used to being greeted with a romantic, 'Hello gorgeous!' This time, it was a flat disinterested, 'Hi.' The indifference level in his voice made Amelia more worried as she anxiously asked her boyfriend if he was okay. Without waiting for his response, she inquired if he had sent her the text message ending their relationship. Amelia did not get any answer to either of her questions. All she could hear was dead silence on the other end of the line. That made her agitated, and somewhat frantically, she demanded that he says something.

After what seemed to be endless silence, he finally cleared his voice and said, 'I am no longer interested. I wish to see you no more.' When Amelia was still in shock, he, without any emotions, added: 'Please don't call my number anymore; there is nothing for me and you to talk about.' With that, he hung up.

Amelia looked at the dead silent phone in her trembling hands and her entire body begun to shake. She felt lost and hopeless. She thought that her whole life and future were crumbling. Her trembling legs could no longer support her shaking body, causing her to collapse on the floor. After a while, she managed to drag her weak body to bed.

That night Amelia cried herself to sleep. However, her sleep was interrupted when she remembered how her boyfriend had talked to her with coldness and indifference. She again started to cry. She wished that what was happening to her was a dream. But no, it was not just a bad dream; it was true. It was an unfortunate reality. The relationship with the man she loved so much had suddenly ended. What made her feel more bitter was that he did not bother to give any reasons, explanations, or even excuses for ending the relationship. She felt insulted, used, exploited, taken advantage of and then discarded as is if she was just a piece of rug. These feeling made her cry for several hours before she fell asleep.

When she woke up, she realized that she was too late for work. She decided to call her manager and let him know that she was not feeling well. Before calling, she first went to the bathroom. As she stood in front of the bathroom mirror, she got terrified by her own image. She took some time standing in front of the mirror, staring at her shattered horrifying face. She could not comprehend how one night of grieving had changed her so much. She could see that she was a different person from what she was before.

She stared at her battered face and said, 'If this is what one night of grieving can do to me, nobody will ever want to look at me if I go on like this for another day.' Addressing her wrecked image in the mirror, she said, 'Come on, girl, you can't allow him to do this to you. He can't break your heart in a remorseless manner, and you go on doing this to yourself because of him.' Pointing at her image in the mirror, she said, 'That is not the face I desire to have. Any man who turns my face to look like that is not worth grieving for.'

With that, she rushed to her room, grabbed the phone, and called her manager. Instead of asking for a day off, she apologised and informed the manager that she would arrive late. She explained to him that she had some personal matters that she needed to sort out. After listening to her, the manager thought that whatever Amelia is dealing with must have been severe. Being a precious and reliable employee, the manager told her that she could take a day off and come the next day. However, Amelia responded by saying that she did not need more time because she had sorted it out.

After taking a quick warm shower, she neatly brushed her hair and put on her best office outfit. She slid on her favourite heels and, just before heading for the door, said a short prayer asking God to help her face the day with courage and fill her mind with positive thoughts. Before heading out of the house, she took one more look in the mirror, 'Looking good!' She exhaled as she stepped out confidently, ready to face the world without the baggage of a broken relationship.

I need you to note the point at which Amelia decides and the type of choice she makes. She could have decided to stay in bed the entire day crying over a broken relationship, feeling bitter about her now ex-boyfriend, and feeling hopeless and helpless. She could have chosen to sit on the sofa the entire day and pity herself for how she was treated. She could have spent the day chanting the phrase, *'It is not fair.'* She could have called a friend to sympathise and cry with her. She could have decided to bury her sorrow and pain in smoking and drugs. She could have drowned her anguish in alcohol. She could have even ended it all by putting her life to an end. There is a probability that all the above options crossed her mind. But Amelia was very smart. Despite the crushing emotional pain that she was experiencing, she decided to make a prudent choice even though it was hard. She did not allow herself time to sink further than she had already gone. As soon as she realized that her crisis was beginning to take over her life, she immediately decided to get back control. She did not give the crisis a chance to take over and be in charge. Amelia lived for a calling that was bigger than having a boyfriend.

The nature of your crisis may be fundamentally different from what Amelia faced. However, the principle remains the same; you should never surrender control to a situation.

When you give up control, you never stop sinking. You can

only stay afloat and be able to swim through if you take back charge of your life. It is acceptable to struggle when you are going through a crisis, but it is disastrous to hand over the control button. This is irrespective of how challenging your situation may be. Remaining in charge gives you the advantage of relating to what you cannot change and stay intact.

Being in charge does not mean the absence of struggle; it means remaining hopeful, focused, positive, sober-minded and rational amidst your battles. Hard times will always require you to take hard decisions. However, when you choose not to make a decision during a crisis, other people or circumstances will make one for you. Unfortunately, it may be a decision that you will regret later in life.

CASE ILLUSTRATION ELEVEN: RUTH

I will give brief facts about Ruth. The story of this heroine of selfless service is found in the Bible. Ruth was a beautiful young Moabite woman who, together with Orpah, another Moabite woman, married two brothers. Both their husbands were Elimelech and Naomi's sons, the Jews who had migrated to Moab's land. Unfortunately, crisis struck, and Naomi and her two daughters-in-law lost their husbands in succession. Left without any kinsmen in Moab, Naomi decides to go back to Bethlehem, her homeland. Although both Ruth and Orpah faced a similar crisis, they had different destinies because of their decisions.

When stakes are high, never surrender your prerogative to make life-changing decisions. Despite the fury of the storm that you are going through, it is crucial that you meticulously take your own decision and stand by it. In most cases, the right choice is usually the one that will appear to be less appealing as it will present more challenges.

There is no doubt that the three widows were a close family. Both Ruth and Orpah expressed the desire to go back with their mother-in-law. Thus, the trio started the journey that would be completed by only two because of the hard decisions involved:

'Naomi and her daughters-in-law prepared to return home from there. With her two daughters-in-law, she left the place where she had been living and set out on the road that would take them back to the land of Judah.'

There is no doubt that the two sisters were dealing with the same crisis in a similar setting. However, their defining moment came when their mother-in-law presented a request that would require them to make a choice. Naomi's suggestion presented the two women with an option that was more appealing, more promising, and safer than the alternative of going with her to Bethlehem. With good intentions for their well-being, she asks both young women to go back to their own families and find new husbands.

What fundamentally distinguished Ruth from Orpah was that Orpah allowed her mother-in-law to make a choice for her. The same offer was given to Ruth, but she insisted on making her own choice. Ruth took the less appealing but appropriate choice. It is crucial to take a personal decision when what is at stake defines who you are.

Orpah was pleased with Naomi's choice. By applying common sense, she was likely to have a better future if she followed Naomi's suggestion. She imagined better chances of getting a comfortable home if she went back to her father's house. Also, logically she had better opportunities of getting remarried if she remained among her people. On the other hand, going back with Naomi to Bethlehem would make her a foreigner among the Jews. That would diminish her chances of getting another husband because the Israelites were discouraged from taking Moabite women. It was, therefore, logically sound for Orpah to take Naomi's suggestion and turn back. The choice that Ruth made posed many risks and required her to move from her comfort zone. However, her resolve to do what is right gave her the zeal and stamina to deal with the challenges that she knew lay along the path of faith that she was choosing to take.

Possibilities of comfort, convenience and acceptance should never be your focus when making decisions that define what you believe and stand for. Orpah took the easy option, and that is the last time her name is mentioned in the Bible. On the other hand, Ruth, with awareness, made a hard but right choice. Her resolve not to abandon her mother-in-law are reflected in her oath of love:

'Entreat me not to leave you,
Or to turn back from following you:
For where you go, I will go;
And where you lodge, I will lodge;
Your people shall be my people,
And your God, my God.
Where you die, I will die,
And there will I be buried.
The Lord do so to me, and more also,
If anything, but death parts you and me.'

With these inspirational words, Ruth makes a choice that forever changes her destiny. She withstands the temptation to take the natural and seemingly promising alternative. This one choice turns Ruth from an ordinary poor widow to becoming a legend of unconditional love.

Antidote 4: Accept reality and move forward

At times people fail to achieve because they refuse to acknowledge the reality of the situation. It is impossible to solve any problem that stands in your way unless you recognise that the problem is real. Issues that are not dealt with have the potential to pull you down at any time. Recognising a situation does not mean condoning it or resigning to it; neither does it mean that you are weak or unable. The advantage of acknowledging the presence of a challenge is that you get an opportunity of dealing with it appropriately. If you are facing failure, know that it is okay to fail. What is not okay is to resign to defeat. Many successful people encountered and dealt with failure on their route to success. Therefore, as you ascend to success, the crucial thing is not to never fail but to know how to handle failure. When a crisis hits, it can throw you down. However, the important thing is not that you have fallen; the critical thing is that you realize that you are down and stand on your feet again. Failures are not necessarily people who fail because successful people do fail as well. What turns one into a failure is the inability to successfully stand up again. You cannot recognize the need to stand unless you are aware that you are down.

The point is, be objective, see the reality and deal with it. Wishful thinking can be disastrous in a crisis. What you need to know is that nothing solves itself. If you want a situation resolved, put in efforts to address it. Your disinterest to face your reality will compromise your tenacity to confront it. When you refuse to acknowledge the presence of a problem, you indirectly cut off available help that would have enabled you to deal with the challenge and pull out of it. Defensive statements such as 'I am fine, I am okay, I am doing great, I can manage, don't worry about me' present a front that works against you. I am not saying that you go drumming your need for help to every person that you meet or that you should accept help from every person. That may not be the right thing to do either because some guidance can be destructive. If you desire support, seek it from the right people. When you do not accept the reality of what you are facing, you fail to recognise your fragility and God's ability to carry you through. When you are with God, you can pull out of any situation.

Antidote 5: Set goals that will keep you focused

You are most prone to being distracted when you are going through a crisis. To move from the undesirable situation that you are in, you need to keep a good focus. You need to have the mental ability to sort out issues you can deal with, issues where you need help and things that you cannot change but must soar above.

Some people become chronic failures because of their inability to recognise and address the core causes of their failure. A misguided response to failure will result in a further and more pronounced fiasco. However, when you set goals, they provide you with a logical way to deal with the crisis you are facing and increase your rate and level of recovery.

For instance, if your GP tells you that your weight poses a risk to your life and that it could possibly lead to your premature death, that is a crisis that you may need to set goals for to get out of. After selecting the overall goal, you will need to develop sub-goals that will enable you to achieve your overall goal. For example, it may be necessary to set the number of kilograms you have to drop. You may need to determine the number of times you have to go to the gym every week. You may also need to establish the number of calories you burn each time you go to the gym and limit the number of calories you take each day.

A person who uses an approach with specific success indicators is likely to see the results faster than a person who tries to address a situation without establishing how progress will be assessed. The principle of goal setting applies in addressing any challenge. It is one of the character traits that distinguishes achievers from failures.

Chapter nine

The Potter's house experience

Resilience

In Jeremiah chapter 18, the prophet was asked by God to go to the Potter's house and derive a message from what the Potter was doing. At the Potter's house, Jeremiah saw the Potter working on the wheel, but the pot that he was shaping got marred in his hands. However, the damaged piece was still valuable in the Potter's eyes. So instead of throwing it away, he moulded it into another valuable article.

Although this allegory had a different message to Jeremiah's audience, it presents several valuable lessons that are timelessly relevant in hard times:

The challenges of life can make you feel like you live on a spinning wheel. When you are facing massive hardships, life can seem to be a rollercoaster that never stops. In such situations, it is possible to think that you have lost control of your life. Dealing with unending problems can cause fear, tension, frustration and a state of hopelessness that makes you want to give up the fight.

However, as the Potter never abandons the vessel that is spinning on the spinning wheel, God also keeps His caring eyes on you when you are going through hard times. God uses the very situations that would have broken you to recreate a more beautiful and successful you. At times, it is the hardships that you go through that become the gateway to your success. When you develop resilience and choose not to quit, you come out as a better person. It is the crucibles of life that test the foundations of your values.

To benefit from your spinning experience, you must have the right attitude. It is essential to look at your crucibles with positive lenses and see beyond the unpleasant aspects of what you are undergoing. A positive attitude during a crisis will enable you to preserve hope and keep you focused, irrespective of what is happening. It is that hope that will maintain your courage not to stop seeking the blessings and opportunities that the future holds.

While some of the spinning that you will go through will be out of the reasons beyond your comprehension, at times, the spinning experience can come as a result of making wrong choices. However, even when the spinning is self-caused, your Maker does not discard you away as waste material. He instead seeks to give you another opportunity by re-shaping you into something better. Yes, your vessel may change in the process of reshaping, but He will still curve you into one of His Masterpieces.

Few people will agree that hard times add value to an individual. If clay had feelings, it would never appreciate the spinning phase, yet clay would never change form without the spinning. The spinning begins the process of transforming ordinary clay with no beauty and no value into an excellent piece. Clay that has not been on the potter's wheel is likely to remain a piece of dirt that people can trample on without caring. Spinning makes clay mouldable and shapable into an item of a higher value. The spinning removes the rough patches and makes the clay mouldable into any shape the potter desires for his product. While spinning makes the previously hard clay, soft, it also enables it to attain its in-woven strength and tenacity. That makes an article made up of fragile clay not to crack when subjected to oven heat. Likewise, depending on the attitude you choose when facing the furnace of life, you can come out of your crisis as a stronger and more successful person.

Shielded by the Potter's hands

If you visit a Potter's house, you will notice that when the clay is on the spinning wheel, it will be surrounded by both hands of the Potter for shaping and protecting it. The only time the Potter will remove one of his hands from the clay is when he reaches out to sprinkle some water on the spinning clay to moist it so that it does not crack and is shapable.

When you apply the analogy to your life, you will notice that the spinning experiences that come your way are not in vain. Take a new perspective of looking at challenges, hard times and crisis that happen to you. You will appreciate the lessons, opportunities and even blessings that may result from hard times.

All the challenging experiences you go through in life can refine your character and prepare you for higher success. However, as already pointed out, the outcome of what you go through will be dictated by the perspective you choose. A similar experience applied to two different individuals with different mindsets can make one emerge as a successful person and the other as a failure. Therefore, you need to guard against the 'surface view syndrome', which can blur your eyes from seeing the treasures underneath what you are going through. To benefit from your spinning experience, you need to adapt the 'miner's perspective' of looking beyond what is presented on the top and dig out what is buried underneath your experience.

In the analogy, God is the Potter, and you are the clay. As the Potter never takes his hand from the spinning clay, so does God. Even though you may at times feel hopeless and alone, God is still right there. His protective arms are ever surrounding you. You may not feel His presence, especially when the spinning goes madly fast, but He is always there. When the heat and the spinning are too much, He pours cooling mercies on you so that you are not consumed by what you are going through.

No matter how intense your spinning gets, it is safer to remain in the Potter's hands than trying to fix things your way. When you get marred on your own, you lose your value. But when you get marred in His hands, He increases your value by shaping you into something better according to the plans He has for your life.

'For I know the plans I have for you, declares the Lord. Plans to prosper you and not to harm you plans to give you hope and a future.' [32]

As you pursue success, things may not always go your way or according to plan. There are times when dreams will crumble and projects miserably fail. Some situations will overwhelm you and make you feel that you can do nothing to spring back. There are moments when you may think that your life is over. Amidst such situations, you need to remember that you still have one asset: your character. You can use that to rebuild your life from nothing to unlimited success. Your character is an asset that can give you a higher value even when everything else has crushed. Success begins in your mind, and the starting point is where you are.

Do not wait for tomorrow. Just start on it, and do not quit.

Endnotes

1. Reader's Digest Oxford Complete Wordfinder. A Unique and Powerful Combination of Dictionary and Thesaurus page 237
2. Galatians 5:22
3. Revelation 14:13
4. 1Corinthians 12:4-7
5. Colossians 3:23
6. The Collins Paperback English Dictionary Completely New Edition page 798
7. Https//www.cdc.gov/ncbddd/disability and health/disability.html
8. Https//www.cdc.gov/ncbddd/disability and health/disability.html
9. 1 Samuel 10:22-23
10. 1 Samuel 10:27
11. Numbers 12:3
12. Philippians 4:8
13. https//www/who.int>mental health
14. Mathew 6:14-15
15. 1 Samuel 30:6 (KJV)
16. Romans 5:8
17. John 3:16
18. Proverbs 14:23
19. Colossians 3:23

ENDNOTES

20 Proverbs 28:19-20
21 Proverbs 9:10
22 Top 30 Quotes of GABBY DOUGLAS ttps: www.inspiringquotes.us
23 Philippians 4:13
24 Isaiah 43:2
25 Jeremiah 29:11
26 Amos 3:3
27 Reader's Digest Oxford Complete Word finder (a unique and powerful combination of dictionary and thesaurus)
28 Philippians 4:6-7
29 ibid
30 Hebrews 11:1
31 Esther 4:16

Your reflections

Your reflections

DEVELOPING THE CHARACTER OF SUCCESS

Your reflections